ST. MARY'S UNIVERSITY COLLEGE LIBRARY
A COLLEGE OF THE QUEENS UNIVERSITY OF BELFAST

Tel. 028 90268237
Web site www.stmarys-belfast.ac.uk
email: library@stmarys-belfast.ac.uk

Fines are charged for overdue and recalled books not returned by notified date.
You will be notified by email of the new date for Recalled books.

Date Due	Date Due	Date Due

Realising Potential
complementary schools in the UK

Tözün Issa and Claudette Williams

Trentham Books
Stoke on Trent, UK and Sterling, USA

Trentham Books Limited
Westview House   22883 Quicksilver Drive
734 London Road   Sterling
Oakhill   VA 20166-2012
Stoke on Trent   USA
Staffordshire
England ST4 5NP

First published 2009

British Library Cataloguing-in-Publication Data
A catalogue record for this book is available from the British Library

ISBN: 978 1 85856 379 4

The authors and Trentham Books thank Sarah Cartwright, consortium manager, our languages project, Ann Carlisle and Teresa Tinsley of CILT for permission to reproduce sections of the CILT Report 2007

Thanks to Steve Smyth for the photograph included in the cover design.

Thanks to Alison Hatt for her valuable suggestions and for proof reading.

Tözün would like to thank the CILT project team: Sarah Minty, Uvanney Maylor, Kuyok Kuyok and Alistair Ross, Institute of Policy Studies in Education (IPSE) London Metropolitan University.

Claudette would like to thank all the Complementary schools staff who participated in our research and special thanks to the Directors and heads or schools who were so generous in giving their time and perspective on their school and the development and role of complementary education in England.

Designed and typeset by Trentham Print Design Ltd, Chester and printed in Great Britain by Cpod Ltd, Trowbridge.

Contents

Introduction

Complementary schools (CS) are voluntary institutions. Also called community or supplementary schools, each one serves a specific linguistic, religious or cultural community (Martin *et al*, 2004). The terminology changes in line with the changing functions and the way they are perceived by the communities running them. The term 'supplementary' is now inadequate and 'community schools' misleading, as it describes certain state schools. 'Complementary' is the appropriate term for these organisations, reflecting the way they support what goes on in mainstream schools and their role in enhancing children's learning.

This book is the outcome of the London Community Schools Project, a research project which explored the multiplicity of functions of these dynamic voluntary institutions and the ways in which they serve the specific needs of their communities. The key issue for ethnic minority communities is improving their children's attainment and this is what characterises the schools. The book examines the changing role of complementary schools in affecting their pupils' learning. The authors of this book both have extensive personal experiences of community schools in London. We taught in them for years and we have served on their management boards.

Community schools in the UK fall into two broad categories: those established for the African Caribbean communities to compensate for the poor provision and the racism their children experience in mainstream schools, and those set up to maintain the languages and cultures of linguistic minority migrant groups.

We did the research together, drawing on our many contacts and the book describes our findings. But we each have inside experience of one of the categories: Tözün of language schools, since Turkish complementary schools typify such provision, and Claudette of African Caribbean schools. We have changed the names of the people we interviewed and the children and also the names of the schools.

There are nearly 1000 complementary schools in London alone, some dating back to the 19th century. The key question we hoped to illuminate through this research was what actually went on in these schools. Can children's experiences in them be utilised to help children progress in mainstream schools? We had little to go on as there is very little research on complementary schools. We hope that this book will fill the gap and capture a picture of the range of community schools serving their communities in the UK today, so that the providers and the teachers in mainstream schools can enrich their understanding of the present scene and think about how to maximise provision for the pupils.

We predicted that we would find schools performing a wide range of functions and this was indeed the case. We found that many have moved away from offering traditional mother tongue instruction and now provide support in the national curriculum (NC), Religious instruction and educating their pupils about their cultural roots. We had expected there to be different combinations – and this book shows how many variations there are in the type of provision the schools offer.

Part One begins with an overview of the scene and goes on to describe the schools we examined. Chapter 1 discusses the historical background: migration patterns, the factors affecting migration and the response of the receiving country. We trace the origins and development of an educational provision that ran outside and parallel to mainstream provision.

In Chapter 2 we look at what is happening currently at these schools. We outline the types of complementary schools and their varied functions and discuss recent projects on complementary schools. Chapter 3 sets out our research methodology and procedures in a systematic way and lists the key findings of our LCSP research. Chapter 4 concentrates specifically on the language schools in our study, and in Chapter 5 Claudette explores the African Caribbean schools.

Part Two introduces the CILT Report, which ran alongside ours and whose findings illuminate our own. In Chapter 6 we outline the CILT project, its scope and research methods. Chapter 7 describes the CS schools examined in the CILT project and introduces their teachers and Chapter 8 describes their qualifications and their career aspirations.

Part Three paints a picture of the people who manage and teach in complementary schools and looks at how their careers might progress. Chapter 9 evaluates the findings of our project, the London Community Schools Project, and in the concluding chapter we make recommendations drawn from both the studies featured in the book. Complementary schools are evolving fast, as this book shows, and we suggest how the teachers who are doing so much for their pupils can be enabled to develop their professional careers and make their schools even better.

PART ONE
Complementary Schools in Britain

1

Setting the scene: the background to complementary schools in the UK

We begin by considering the social and political factors affecting the formation of the complementary schools, the patterns of migration and settlement of particular communities. Although we acknowledge that each community, each family or indeed each individual has a story to tell about Britain, we decided that in order to support our empirical investigation it would be useful to start from the two broad perspectives, namely the African Caribbean and the linguistic minority experiences. Throughout the book we hope to show readers a correlation between the particular community and individual experiences and the emerging patterns in migration. It was a common story for all: how to survive in a hostile and inherently racist country.

History and migration

Britain has always been a country of newcomers. Records show the presence of minority communities dating back to the 12th Century. There is a story behind every migration: often communities were escaping religious or political persecution or migrating for economic advancement or better educational opportunities. Settlement followed similar patterns: the formation of closely-knit communities concerned to preserve their cultural and linguistic characteristics as a defence against hostility and racism. The period following the end of the Second World War was marked by significant migration to the UK from the former Crown Colonies.

1

Britain has not been short of overseas settlers. Winder (2004) reports that there were French Jews in London, Lincoln, York and Norwich in the 12th Century, before their formal expulsion *en masse* in 1290. Henry VIII invited skilled ironworkers from Germany to pound steel in the Royal Armoury in Sussex. Under King Edward VI Flemish, Dutch and French Protestants flourished in England, setting up businesses and their own churches. But mass emigration from France of Protestants did not happen until 1572 when the Huguenots were forced to flee in great numbers, followed by another mass wave in 1674 when hostilities 'bubbled to the surface again' (*ibid*:79).

Winder relates that the Elizabethan age brought Italian musicians and financiers as well as Africans 'pressed by the first piratical stirrings of the slave trade' (2004:3). The accession of William of Orange to the English throne in 1688 pleased the Huguenots and other Protestants in the country. It also ensured the entry into England of the new Dutch elite, who brought with them engineers, clockmakers, goldsmiths and artists. One of the most famous immigrants of them all, George I, was a German and by the middle of the 18th century, when his son George II was monarch, there were 5,000 Germans in Britain (*ibid*:109).

In the latter part of the 18th Century, Britain's fortunes were founded on slavery. The *Morning Gazette* of 1765 claimed there were as many as 30,000 'negro servants' in London alone (*ibid*, p.129).

With the abolition of slavery in 1833 and the emancipation of Catholics (1829) and Jews (1835), Britain in the 19th century began to attract entrepreneurs, revolutionaries and skilled workers from all over Europe. Guiseppe Mazzini, chief architect of the liberation of Italy, came to Britain after his expulsion from Switzerland in 1836. It was a similar story for Kossuth, who had to flee Hungary. Karl Marx worked and wrote his *Das Capital* in London. A cluster of expatriates formed around these leading figures (*ibid*:150). Britain was living up to its reputation as the 'Workshop of Europe'.

At the end of the Second World War nearly 9000 Ukrainian refugees arrived in Britain, displaced by the advancing Red Army as Ukraine was engulfed by the USSR (Haxell, 1979). Polish speakers have arrived in the UK in waves over the last three hundred years. The first began in the late 18th century when Poland was partitioned by Austria, Prussia and

Russia. The wartime *Emigracja* (emigration) (1940-1950) of members of the Polish Armed Forces and their families and political prisoners from concentration camps in Germany and Russia brought an estimated 165,000 additional Poles to the UK. Small numbers of new migrants arrived in the wake of the Solidarity Movement in the 1980s. Following Poland's entry into the European Union, the UK proved for some years to be a popular destination. At the time of writing there are an estimated 750,000 people with Polish connections in the UK. They range from the grandchildren of those who came in the wartime *Emigracja* to the recent arrivals from Poland in search of work.

During the 1990s war-torn zones in the Balkans forced refugees from Bosnia and Kosova to flee to the UK. Similarly, the lifting of the iron curtain enabled peoples of Russia, Romania and more recently Bulgaria, with its imminent European accession to the European Union, to seek new opportunities in Britain.

New Commonwealth immigration

It is a common assumption that emigration from the ex-British Colonies officially began in 1948 when an old Second World War German cruiser *Empire Windrush* brought in 492 'intending immigrants' from Kingston, Jamaica (Jones, 1977:122). But the Black presence in Britain goes back to before the days of slavery. There was migration from these Colonies well before they gained their independence. People from the Indian Sub-continent, Cypriots and Maltese arrived in Britain during the period between the two world wars and some before the First World War.

The most noticeable migration after the Second World War was from the West Indies followed by migration from India and Pakistan. Jones (1977) cites 1961 census figures confirming total emigration from the New Commonwealth as 522,933. The 1962 *Commonwealth Immigration Act* was designed to restrict migration by claiming to allow only the workforce needed to come into Britain. Vouchers were issued to bring people into the country as the 'needed skilled force'. Each family could bring one member of their family with them and this enabled a considerable number of skilled workers and professionals, particularly from the state of Gujarat to enter the UK (Desai, 1963).

In 1971 the political upheavals culminating in events in Pakistan became a catalyst in the migration of semi-skilled and unskilled villagers from what had become the newly founded state of Bangladesh (Khan, 1976). Although the first mass migration from the former British Raj came in the form of Sikhs from the Punjab and Hindus from the Gujarat regions after the partition in 1947, the first Indian Sikhs who arrived in Britain during the 1920s were members of the small Bhara caste who made their living as pedlars (Taylor, 1976).

In 1979 Britain took nearly 10,000 Vietnamese refugees from the transit camps in Hong Kong and their numbers reached 16,000 by the end of 1982 (Taylor, 1988). The military rule in Turkey caused a sizeable population of Turkish professionals and Turkish speaking Kurds to seek refuge in the UK (Issa, 2005). With the arrival of refugees from Iraq and Iran the Kurdish population in Britain rose to 300,000. Personal discussion with Yashar Ismailoğlu, then head of *Halkevi*, the Kurdish Cultural Centre in East London during a visit in 2005, confirmed this as the official number.

The reasons for migration differed. For some, Britain was nothing more than a temporary home until they earned enough money to ensure a comfortable life back home. For others there was no question of return for fear of religious or political persecution. But survival in a foreign and often hostile environment depended on the preservation of cultural, religious and linguistic values. In practice this meant passing them on to the next generation irrespective of future plans.

The African Caribbean Story

Black people's presence in Britain fits into the ebb and flow of immigration and settlement of peoples into the lands that comprise the UK. It pre-dates Elizabethan England. It is recorded that during times of economic hardship Queen Bess decreed that 'Blackamoors' be banished from her realm and sent to Africa (Fryer, 1984). As Dabydeen (1987) point out: Hogarth's depictions of black people amongst the working classes of 18th Century Britain are made very visible by their blackness.

The recent bicentenary commemoration of the abolition of the Atlantic Slave Trade in 1807 has afforded high visibility and heightened the acknowledgement of the legacy of African slavery. The fabric of 'Britishness' is imbued with the black African legacy.

4

The North Atlantic slave trade swelled the numbers of black people amongst the British poor. The sizable black populations in ports like London, Cardiff, Bristol and Liverpool built up as a result of Britain's highly successful commercial activities during the 17th and 18th centuries and the slavery in mainland Britain (Fryer, 1984:191-236). The *Morning Gazette* of 1765 reported that London had a population of 30,000 negro servants (Winder, 2004:129). Some of these servants would have been chattel slaves brought and sold by British merchants in British ports. Groups of sailors, the lascars, who settled in port cities, came from India and China. Indian women were a visible feature of the black port pattern of settlement. As Rozina Visram wrote:

> Some Asians, such as servants and *ayahs* (nannies), were brought to Britain to serve the personal needs and whims of their masters and mistresses. Many were sent back to India when no longer required, but others remained to serve in the households of wealthy India-returned memsabs. Like African servants, Indians were fashionable in the eighteenth century as status symbols. Some servants were sold or given away, some ran away to escape maltreatment. (1993:168)

By the 18th century the black population in Britain impinged on all aspects of national life. The National Archives website concludes its 'Work in the Community' section by stating that:

> By the mid-eighteen century African and Asian people had become part of the fabric of British society. The history of White employers cannot be separated from the history of the man and woman who worked for them. African, Caribbean and Asian people lived and laboured beside English washerwomen, domestic maids, cooks, sailors and soldiers. (http://www.national archives.gov.uk)

This quotation shows acknowledgement of the presence of black people, but only in the poor and working classes. But it is important not to forget that black people were also present and visible within the gentry and aristocracy. Rodgers, the American Black historian (1966) identified black people in all strata of European life, such as Queen Charlotte, Royal Consort and wife of George III, who is described as being of African (Moorish) descent. The National Trust recently ran an exhibition on the black African legacy in Britain, featuring the mixed heritage of Dido Elizabeth Belle, related to Lord Mansfield of Kenwood (National Trust, 2007; Sherwood, 2007).

Ignatius Sancho (1729-1780) was recognised as part of the social and intellectual fabric of high society in London. Dubbed the 'man of letters', he had his portrait painted by his friend and sponsor Thomas Gainsbrough. Today the painting hangs in the National Portrait Gallery in London alongside another daughter of the realm, Mary Seacole. This Jamaican nurse made her own way to the Crimean War to nurse British soldiers in her own hospital alongside Florence Nightingale (Dabydeen, 1994; Seacole, 1990).

Neither should popular Victorian novels which informed people's imagination about the black presence be overlooked. They tell stories about young men going off to the colonies, some to assuage their wrongdoings, or to oversee their plantation – to replenish it with new African slaves, perhaps – and others to make their fortunes and return to capture the heroine's affection (Dabydeen, 1985 cites *inter alia*, Jane Austen and Charlotte Bronte).

The unseen first Mrs Rochester in Charlotte Bronte's *Jane Eyre*, a black (Creole) woman from the West Indies, was locked away in the attic (Bronte, 1847). Was this because of her madness or her blackness?

I share the frustration of many regarding the collective amnesia of the long imperialist history of black people in Britain, especially when our presence in society is reduced and dated to the disembarkation of black men (and one woman) from the SS Empire Windrush, as it docks at Tilbury In 1949. The steamship Empire Windrush, it was reported, '...brought the first generation of migrant workers from the Caribbean to England...' (www.icons.org.uk/theicons/collection/ss-wndrush. biography) but this was not the whole story.

The arrival of SS Windrush did indeed symbolise the beginning of a large post Second World War migration of black people from British Colonies to Britain, 'the motherland'. However the long established black presence, replenished by demobbed black soldiers, students, political activists and black intellectuals (see Perkins and Mavinga McKenzie, 1992; Schwarz, 2002; Levy, 2005) would help fashion and change the colonial relationship of the motherland and her subjects. The iconic status given to the West Indians arriving on the Windrush helped to minimise the significance of the struggles and experiences of the existing black communities in Britain. As Brown (2005) pointed out:

...the educational disadvantages experienced by descendents of black African Caribbean children are shared by indigenous black children from Liverpool's old established port communities.

Contemporary experience of education, which is the concern of this book, points to areas of British life in which black children and their families are disfranchised from the full benefits of state education. During the 1960s the Caribbean community became very concerned about the poor education provided to black children. The growth of black supplementary schools can be marked from this period. Bernard Coard's seminal work *How the West Indian Child is Made Educationally Subnormal in the British School System* (1971) exposed and documented the scandalously discriminatory and destructive education experienced by many black children.

A migrant's story – Claudette Williams relates her experience

The mass migration of young men and women from the Caribbean to Britain during the 1960s meant that many children were left behind with grandparents, aunts or older siblings. Many extended families were sustained by money sent back home, supplemented by seasonal parcels of clothing, shoes and toys, carrying high status amongst peers because they came from England.

Black migrants from the Caribbean expected to come to England, 'work some money', and go back home. The planned response to the call for labour was never to stay and live in Britain. The tradition of migration and return was an identified feature of Caribbean migratory labour: workers who went to build the Canal in Panama and farm workers who went to North America, Cuba and other Caribbean islands intended to find work and return home with money. My parents, like many from Jamaica, came to England in the late 1950s and 60s. My father came first and worked as a painter, factory worker and eventually as a ticket collector on London Transport. He left behind four children, the youngest only three months old. My mother came in 1961 to join him in Brixton, London, where a Jamaican community had established itself. Work was obtainable and rooms could be rented. My mother first lived in a room on Shakespeare Road in Brixton Hill, sharing kitchen, bathroom and outside toilet with four other couples and single men. At that time no children lived in the household. However as Parliament began to fashion the Commonwealth Immigration Act (1962), placing restrictions and creating categories determining who would be eligible to immigrate, black workers with children back home began to organise to have their children 'sent up' to England. The rush was on to 'beat the ban'. As Vertovec noted:

> ...by far the greatest influx of West Indians took place initially prior to implementation of the 1962 Commonwealth Immigration Act, when thousands migrated for fear of having the door permanently shut'. (1993:170)

My arrival in England was as a consequence of my parents' efforts to beat the ban, even though we did not arrive until 1965 (see case study below).

The first focus of Caribbean immigration was to rebuild the British economy and satisfy the demand for labour. The initial intention was to work, save some money and return home. These desires shifted and formed what was considered the second wave of mass post war immigration, propelled by the threat of exclusion. The arrival of children and extended families marked the shift to establish permanent homes in Britain.

My mother left my younger brother and me in the care of my paternal aunt, who had three other children around the same age. Other members of my father's family lived in the adjacent yards, and took responsibility for all the children whenever an adult was absent. Regular remittances supplemented by parcels of clothing, shoes and toys were 'sent down from England'. Parcels sent by my mother engendered both excitement and anxiety for me, especially about getting new shoes. My rapidly growing feet caused me constant grief. Between the time my string measurements were posted to England and my shoes lovingly bought and parcelled off to Jamaica some months had elapsed and, alas, my feet had grown. My new robust sensible Clarks' girl shoes would be too tight, and could not fit my feet. My shoes would be passed on to a cousin and I would be left with an ill-fitting adult hand-me-down pair.

After Jamaica gained its independence from England in 1962, it became a general expectation that if you had family in England you would be leaving to go and join your parents. Soon, leaving Jamaica became every child's fantasy, heightened by the lack of emotional nurturing. The rumours started in my family during the late summer of 1965. There was no preparation for the soon to start school year, no buying of school books or clothes. Our suspicions were confirmed when we had to make the trip to Kingston to have photographs taken for passports: our parents were not coming back but we were going to England.

We arrived in England on November 16 1965, a cold, dark, grey winter's day. During the following week, my mother enrolled us in the 'good' primary school, Kings Acre, where I spent one year. I was allocated a seat in the back of the class, from where I tried to understand the language of the class and my south London classmates. The first English word I learned was 'pardon' because whenever I spoke I was met with the response 'Pardon?' So I quickly learnt to adjust my Jamaican accent to south London English. The academic demands of school work were slight as I had covered much of the syllabus back in Jamaica. I did not find the work hard or challenging, I simply got on with doing it again.

I was astonished by my classmates' general lack of geographical and historical knowledge. They had little knowledge of the world, where to find countries on the globe or world map. My brother and I could locate almost any country on a map and name the country and major cities. We could list all the kings and queens of England. Yet my classmates had no idea of the West Indies or where to find the islands on a map. Jamaica was synonymous with mainland Africa and all their stereotyping of Africa and Africans came to the fore. I was astonished by their ignorance and my teacher's indifference to my own knowledge. I remember how, because I had already covered the mathematics we were doing in class, I was able to complete the work ahead of the others – and how my teacher dismissed my efforts. My geographical and historical knowledge was likewise disregarded.

* * *

Complementary schools: a historical overview

Complementary schools go back to the mid-1800s, when a sizeable Italian community was established in Clerkenwell in London, with its own church and a hospital (King, 1977a). Many early complementary schools were formed primarily for retention of language and cultural values. A leading Republican intellectual from Rome and later influential Italian politician, Mazzini, helped establish the first Italian school and started teaching there in 1837 (Walker, 1982). In London's docklands a community school was set up in the late 19th Century to teach the children of Chinese dockers (Issa, 2002).

The number of complementary schools increased from the 1950s onwards with the arrival of communities from the New Commonwealth. The first Greek Cypriot school opened in Kentish Town in London at much the same time, in response to pressures from the Greek Orthodox Church and the Greek Embassy (Tansley, 1986). The first Ukrainian mother tongue school was set up during the 1950s and was well established by the 1960s (Khan, 1980). The first Turkish school was set up in 1959 to promote 'mother tongue teaching and preservation of the Turkish culture' (Taylor, 1988). Other communities followed suit.

There appeared to be a pattern to setting up the complementary schools: communities would follow their compatriots into urban areas where they would find employment in local economies. Thus the community would be increased. Soon demands from parents and community members would prompt activists and leaders in the community to seek ways of establishing a school. The schools for the Bangladeshi and Vietnamese communities during the 1970s followed a similar pattern.

The complementary schools were set up for more than just the maintenance of cultural, linguistic values and ethnic identity (Taylor, 1988). Several Black complementary schools were a direct response to Government policies and so-called 'compensatory initiatives' to tackle black underachievement (Plowden Report DES, 1967). As discussed later, some complementary schools are moving away from their traditional language only policies to multiple functions in order to serve the needs of their communities. In the next section we explore how what started as a response developed into a co-ordinated effort in the form of African Caribbean complementary schools.

African Caribbean Complementary Schools

Education has always been a burning issue for Black women. Viewed, in the aftermath of slavery, as virtually the only means for our children and us to escape the burden of poverty and exploitation, it was regarded in the Caribbean as a kind of liberation (Bryant *et al*, 1985).

African Caribbean parents' instincts were to trust the system and to assume its good will. In the circumstances it was a reasonable reaction. 'Their own education, after all, had been British' wrote the Philips brothers (1998). This trust and aspiration soon dissipated, as an already class based education system adopted and implemented a racialised response to the schooling of black children. There was a delay before parents realised the full implications of what was happening to black children in local schools. A collective community response to discriminatory education practices was mobilised by community activists such as John La Rose and Waveney Bushell in north London and Jessica and Eric Huntley in west London. The blatantly racist proposals the Haringey Education Committee presented in the Doulton Report, in an attempt to justify the introduction of dispersal of black children, claimed that:

> On a rough calculation half the immigrants will be West Indians at seven of the eleven [*secondary*] schools, the significance of this being the general recognition that their IQs will work out below their English contemporaries. Thus academic standards will be lower in schools where they form a large group. (Doulton Report, 1969:para11)

This provided the catalyst for Waveney Bushell, chair of the North London West Indian Association (NLWIA) to issue statements condemning the proposals and mobilising parents and the community to resist the Education Committee's proposal. She wrote:

> It is necessary to state quite unequivocally that the NLWIA, its members and supporters continue to be opposed to the proposals for banding... we also need to state that West Indians and their offspring will not be entirely satisfied until the offensive and dangerous remarks about their children's capacity as stated or implied in those documents are fully withdrawn. (Bushell, 1969)

The NLWIA's statement was significant. It acknowledged that black children were indeed underachieving in Haringey schools but argued that what was needed to stop the decline in reading standards was not the dispersal of black children but the need to employ black teachers in the schools. These personnel, Bushnell argued, 'will be emotionally and culturally attuned to West Indian students and their needs in school'.

Reading tests were culturally biased against black children and fed into existing pejorative stereotypes. This documented articulated issues and demands that Bernard Coard (1971) would later expand on as a result of the research called for in the NLWIA's proposal.

In West London the thrust for supplementary schools and the campaign about poor educational provision was further heightened when it was realised that children who were being allocated to 'Special schools' were in fact being sent to schools for educationally subnormal. Eric Huntley described how:

> ... parents thought that their child is going to a Special School, then they're going to a good school, because in the Caribbean, when we say 'special' we mean 'good'. But then we realised it wasn't so and it was at that period that all that took place ...when a group of us came together and organised a group called Caribbean Education and Community Workers Association. (CECWA; quoted in Philips and Philips, 1998:257)

CECWA called attention to the poor education children were receiving and to the culturally biased tests used to diagnose and allocate black children to the 'special schools'. Communities were further mobilised and the national campaigns launched when Coard's research was published.

How the West Indian child is made Educational Subnormal by the British Education System (Coard, 1971) demonstrated that the miseducation and widescale diagnosis of black children as ESN was much more extensive and existed at national level.

Coard reported that

> ... disproportionate numbers of West Indian children are in the lowest streams of secondary schools; thousands have been placed in ESN schools, where the authorities themselves now admit they do not belong; in some boroughs they are being bussed from their neighbourhood to a far distant school, the children have been banded – or branded – about the school in various boroughs, on the assumption that they are of 'low intelligence' and culturally deprived; and so must be spread in twos and threes throughout the school system to prevent 'standards' being lowered'. (1971:56)

The situation demanded immediate action and parents had to be instrumental in making changes. Coard recommended direct interaction and intervention in schools and the curriculum but, more importantly, energy was also directed to 'things we can do for ourselves' such as set up black nurseries and to...

> Start up supplementary schools in whatever part of London or Britain we live, in order to give our children additional help in the subjects they need. These classes can be held on evenings and Saturday mornings. We should recruit all our Black students and teachers for the task of instructing our children. Through these schools we hope to make up for the inadequacies of the British school system, and for its refusal to teach our children our history and culture. We must not sit idly by while they make ignoramuses of our children, but must see to it that by hook or by crook our children get the best education they are capable of! (p52)

Supplementary schools must be staffed with black teachers, because they will be attuned to the cultural and linguistic norms of the children. A relevant curriculum must reflect the global and historical inter-relationships between Britain and the rest of the world, one in which:

> Black history and culture ie the history of Black people throughout the Caribbean, the Americas, Africa and Asia, should be made part of the curriculum *for all* schools, for the benefit of the Black and the white children. (p52)

Coard goes on to assert that a curriculum without this kind of knowledge base would 'constitute nothing short of criminal negligence (or prejudice) in the education sphere' (p52).

An Afrocentric curriculum, as advocated by Coard, would have cognitive as well as psychological positive outcomes for black children. Further momentum was added to Coard's call for this kind of self help, grass roots community organisation, as it intersected with the rise of the Black Power movement in the early 1970s. The realisation that direct action was required in the area of education strengthened and became interlinked with other social and political demands being made for social justice and against racism. However a key issue still remained: how to finance these schools.

Financial support for complementary schools
The initial funding for the schools came from the communities themselves, often in the form of donations from parents, community organisations and the embassies, which supported the schools with

teachers sent from the 'mother country' (Taylor, 1988). Today more and more schools are asking for a small subscription fee from parents to offset their expenses and pay the staff who are not employed directly by the embassies.

Government support for complementary provision began in the 1970s after the European Economic Community (EEC) declaration support- ing the maintenance of the mother tongue of migrant children for 'the case of eventual return to the country of origin' (Issa, 2002). There was initial resistance from the British government on grounds that the situation of the minorities did not constitute 'migrant' status. Even- tually pressure from Europe and community groups in the UK forced the Government to back down. By 1975, the Bullock Report was urging schools not to expect their pupils to leave their language and culture on the school threshold.

Several Government funded initiatives actively supported mother tongue provision, such as the Bradford Mother Tongue Project which ran from 1977-1982 (see Klein, 1982) and later the Linguistic Minorities Project (see Stubbs, 1985) among them. Some local authorities (LAs) provided mother tongue support as part of the normal teaching timetable in schools. The Inner London Education Authority (ILEA) was particularly active, supporting both Language schools and African Caribbean Saturday schools in London, but it was abolished in 1990. Today, with the marketisation of education, the financial burden of sup- porting complementary schools has once again fallen to the communi- ties, as more and more schools are told by their local authorities that the premises will in future be charged for. Today very few LAs support their local community schools.

This chapter traced the patterns of migration and the historical factors that affected them. In the next chapter we look at what is currently hap- pening in the schools. We consider various types of complementary schools and their differing functions and explore some recent research into complementary schools.

2

Current provision

In this chapter we explore the situation of complementary schools in the UK today and the Government's position on them. We provide an overview of current provision within the complementary sector and look at existing policy and guidelines. It is useful to identify common trends and practices before examining them in detail. We consider financial matters as well as issues such as training and the role of the parents. We begin with the government.

There is ample evidence relating to the government's interest in complementary schools. The Department of Children Schools and Families (DCSF) website lists the key principles and suggestions on the importance of maintaining links between mainstream and community groups. The QCA website lists essential components as well as educational justifications for the Government's interest (http://www.qca/org.uk). It gives a key message that 'a school's link with neighbourhood communities begins in the classroom' (p2).

The government's first serious step towards supporting the complementary schools sector came with its fairly recent decision to fund the National Resource Centre (NRC) for Supplementary Schools in London. This had been running as the only resource centre for supplementary and mother tongue schools in England for ten years, before merging with *ContinYou* in 2006.

The centre lists its aims as working with supplementary school leaders, education professionals and campaigners to:

- ▓ raise standards in supplementary education
- ▓ raise the profile of supplementary schools and what they can achieve
- ▓ raise funds for supplementary schools

The NRC works with a range of partners in Coventry, Lewisham, Barnet and Ealing and acts as a delivery partner in twelve other London boroughs. It supports complementary schools applying for Local Network Funds in Enfield, Hackney, Islington, Camden, Tower Hamlets, Westminster, Haringey, Hammersmith and Fulham, Kensington and Chelsea, Wandsworth, Merton and Sutton. The DfES funded the NRC until the Paul Hamlyn Foundation took over in March 2008 (http://www.continyou.org.uk/content).

In other boroughs local authority funding for complementary schools is patchy and this is reflected in the different local arrangements. For example, while a Turkish community School in Walthamstow pays an annual rent of £10,000 to a local secondary school for the use of their school premises on Saturdays, a Gujarati school in Brent pays a daily fee of £450. In some authorities such as Lewisham, some schools are given moderate funding to meet their expenses, mainly for the hire of premises. But the funding from LAs is limited. For example the Learning Trust in Hackney, though a strong supporter of community education, can only fund four out of fourteen established Turkish complementary schools. On the other hand, the larger authority of Birmingham put aside an annual grant of £191,910 in the 2003-2004 financial year alone to support 107 community complementary schools (averaging £1250-£3000 per school) to cover tutor fees, equipment and material costs and rent. (http://www.bgfl.org/services/suppsch/stats.htm)

The main source of income for most complementary schools remains the donations and annual membership fees paid by the parents.

The NRC has carried out a review of language teaching and complementary schools in Lambeth, while in Hackney it has set up a quality inspection programme of local complementary schools in collaboration with the Learning Trust, the 'not for profit' organisation which runs education services for Hackney.

In addition the NRC runs a Quality Framework programme. Devised in 2005-2006 through consultation between the Resource Unit for Supplementary Schools and Pan London, a non-governmental organisation working in partnership with other institutions, it aimed to develop the 'first nationally recognised quality mark for supplementary education' (http://www.continyou.org.uk) and provide complementary schools with awards for services to the voluntary sector. The Quality Framework pilot worked with fourteen supplementary schools in six local authorities and was supported by a small grant from the DCSF. The Framework enables schools services to be publicly promoted and recognised. It also provides a structure for them to develop and strengthen their own practices. In short, it provided motivational guidance. The Framework contains:

- three Areas of Achievement – teaching and learning, management, planning and partnerships
- nine Quality Standards – with clear descriptors and evidence lists at each level to help schools make objective judgements
- three Levels of Award: Bronze, Silver and Gold

The Framework is implemented in six stages:

Stage 1: Identification: The LA's supplementary schools co-ordinator works with local supplementary schools to identify which schools would be willing to participate in the pilot

Stage 2: Pre-assessment (once identified, the mentor helps schools through the process of self-assessment)

Stage 3: Evidencing attainment (the mentor helps the school to develop a portfolio of evidence to support that self-assessment)

Stage 4: Recognition meetings (selected mentors scrutinise evidence from portfolios and hear presentations from three or four schools)

Stage 5: Moderation (to ensure consistency of assessment)

Stage 6: Schools are notified of their award at the level of Bronze, Silver or Gold (http://www.bgfl.org/services/ suppsch/stats.htm)

The impact of complementary schools

There are estimated to be over 2,200 complementary and mother tongue schools in England alone. They are run by community groups and housed in a variety of venues such as mosques, churches, temples, gurdwaras, community centres, libraries and other public buildings with large rooms (http://www.qca.org.uk/10007).

As observed in Reay and Mirza's (1997) study, women are visible as organisers and lead in many of the complementary schools. The replies to our questionnaire indicated a number of woman respondents, but we did not inquire about the gender of the staff in schools so whether this is significant would need further investigation.

Although all complementary schools undertake key activities, as shown in our findings in Chapter 3, the degree and complexity of these activities varies from school to school. All schools are concerned with:

- helping pupils with National Curriculum subjects, particularly Mathematics, English, Science and ICT
- enabling pupils to learn about the history and culture of their heritage community and the community in which they live
- teaching pupils their home language as well as other languages of cultural or religious significance.
- enabling children to become successful learners
- engaging parents in their children's schooling

The Multiverse website, an initial teacher education (ITE) professional resource network funded by the Training and Development Agency (TDA) for Schools, highlights the positive outcomes of complementary schools for the children who attend. The website has been developed for teacher educators, student teachers and teachers, in response to newly qualified teachers' request for more support in teaching pupils from minority ethnic backgrounds and those with English as an additional language (www.multiverse.ac.uk)

Multiverse provides resources and considers issues of social class, ethnic, cultural and religious diversity. It lists and analyses how these impact on refugees, asylum seekers, Travellers and Roma communities. The website recognises the positive effects of attending complementary schools and these are highlighted through examples of:

■ *language learning*

- [ ] exploring bilingualism through case studies from various communities

- [ ] improving SATs results for those who attended complementary schools

■ *cultural connections*

- [ ] maintaining children's links with their family and community

- [ ] creating a sense of belonging to a community

- [ ] embedding in pupils a strong sense of identity

■ *reinforcing the mainstream school curriculum*

- [ ] providing additional support for mainstream school learning such as consolidating English literacy and providing support for homework

■ *broadening the curriculum*

- [ ] providing additional music lessons on a range of instruments and lessons on subjects such as singing

- [ ] providing dance lessons and giving performances

- [ ] offering a different context and perspective from mainstream school for children to study history, citizenship, geography and RE (Kenner, 2004).

Students' experiences in complementary schools

The experiences of complementary school students are generally found to be positive. Gregory and Williams (2000) cite an example of a Jewish man who attended a community school as a child in the 1930s and described how his bilingualism helped his acquisition of English in mainstream school. He recalled that...

> At the age of 7, we were learning Hebrew grammar which is far more complicated in many ways than English grammar, so when we were in the English school, adjectives, nouns and verbs, things which non Jewish friends would just be beginning to grapple with were all very natural to us. (2000:91)

In their recent study of two Turkish complementary schools Creese *et al* (2007) offer useful examples of students' views about attending their local community school. Students feel proud about speaking two languages:

> Interviewer: How do you feel about being able to speak Turkish?
>
> Child: I kind of show off to my friends.
>
> Interviewer: You do, how do you show off?
>
> Child: I say 'I know two main languages and I'm learning two more'.
>
> Interviewer: Oh I see, you're adding your German and French as well. So you say 'I am multilingual, I know four languages'. How many languages do they speak?
>
> Child: My friends? they speak one main language
>
> Interviewer: Hhmmm.
>
> Child: Which is English.
>
> Interviewer: Hhh but you have two main languages?
>
> Child: Yeah Turkish and English.
>
> Interviewer: and you're proud about it?
>
> Child: Yeah
>
> (2007:5)

Creese notes how the high achieving children's success is celebrated during assemblies and social occasions such as end of year prize winning ceremonies in both these schools. She observes that 'children's efforts were publicly praised and high achievers were implicitly positioned as role models' (2007:5). The students take visible pride in being able to speak another main language besides English. Creese *et al* point to the children's eagerness to learn another language – something which contradicts 'mainstream narratives of academic failure' (2007:5).

Creese and her colleagues report that students talked about the importance of becoming literate in Turkish and the role of Turkish complementary schools in this process. One girl compared her literacy skills in Turkish and English the following way:

(English translation in brackets)

Child: *Ben de da başka bir dil daha bilirim ve yazabilirim ve çünkü böyle şey yaparım* (I know one more language and I can write it and because I do this)

Interviewer: Gururlanırsın you feel proud any other feelings? (You feel proud, you feel proud, any other feelings?

Child: No

Interviewer: Ok Peki, is this different from your feelings towards English?

Child: *Benim İngilizcede böyle daha çok şey şey yapmam ama böyle İngilizcede çünkü daha çok bilirim İngilizcede ve Türkçe de o kadar böyle İngilizceden daha çok bilmem. Daha çok Türkçe de memnum olurum böyle yazdığımda, çünkü o kadar böyle Turkce de bilirim ama İngilizce de İngilizcede bilirim ama Türkçe de o kadar bilmem.*

(My English I can do a lot more things in English because I know a lot more in English, but in Turkish I don't know as much as I know in English. When I write something in Turkish it pleases me a lot more, because I know that much Turkish)

In another recent research report commissioned by Multiverse, Robertson (2006) looks at how to build links between community languages schools and mainstream schools. She acknowledges the community groups as valuable domains for learning for student teachers, ITE providers and research communities. She examines how they can provide and further develop student teachers' knowledge and understanding of different linguistic, ethnic and cultural groups at KS1 and 2 in mainstream schools. The key objectives of the Multiverse research were:

- ▓ to explore student teachers' perceptions of linguistic minority pupils' learning
- ▓ to find out and examine how ITE providers can support student teachers in teaching pupils of diverse backgrounds
- ▓ to examine how bi/multilingual student teachers can develop new ways in which they make use of their own bilingualism in mainstream schools and within community groups
- ▓ to develop a 'partnership package' specifying how to develop and manage similar projects and to offer this to ITE providers and community language schools via the Multiverse website (www.multiverse.ac.uk).

The report consists of case studies of four student teachers' experiences of their visits to complementary schools in London. Sabia, one of the student teachers, talked about how she might make further use of her experiences after the visit.

> I have always enjoyed having people in the class, and having people from the Turkish or Greek school in the class, and to teach the class something, or to do with the events of the class... Lots of different things, really.

> Yes, I'm more confident in understanding where their languages and their learning come from. So obviously they have an extra strength to their learning. They have more to offer ... I think, having language experiences in which they [bilingual pupils] actually teach the [other] children. ... Not just show and tell time but having exclusive class time, even in literacy, where they can show and express in another language and using different readings. (2006: 12)

When the student teachers were asked about what they learned as the result of their visits they all indicated that this would positively affect their own future practice. They said that they had changed their views about their role as a teacher and also about the terminology used to describe pupils who have English as an additional language (EAL). They said that they had begun to talk about pupils' bilingualism, rather than about EAL or pupils' lack of English.

Sophie was explicit in her reflections on her learning:

> Their strengths, and their languages, you know, you would be able to incorporate into other lessons. It's less scary now. You just think, I'll do that. (p9)

After the visits Louise was already planning how she might use her experiences:

> You could incorporate translations and stuff in the child's language and then they'd feel more included in the lessons... So if you were telling a story you'd have pictures or translations in their language. I'd definitely do that. I never had a chance before. So definitely I'd do that.

> I do see the potential to make the links. You know, just to see the kind of curriculum they're teaching and if there are any cross-curricular links between their curriculum and our curriculum. (p14)

What is really happening in complementary schools?

Both the reports quoted (Creese *et al*, 2007; Robertson, 2006) reveal interesting findings about what is going on inside complementary schools. For a start, both studies highlight the linguistic, cultural and social significance of complementary schools. Learning the language and culture is seen as an important tool for achieving well in the mainstream. Both reports note also the benefits of 'other activities' such as homework clubs to support Maths, English and Science, as well as the folk dancing, music and football activities held mainly in the afternoons. Children's maintenance of their cultural identity was seen by Creese and her colleagues as being interwoven with their understanding of English culture .

Both studies identified the strong parental involvement they found and the way this had added to the cohesiveness of the community. The parents' active participation and their clear interest in their children's education were evident in the parent school association meetings. Creese *et al* give examples in their study which bring home how seriously parents viewed their children's achievement in the education system. There appeared to be well-organised and efficient systems in operation, with active participation by all interested parties. As observed by one of the visitors in Robertson's study: 'They were all, yes, so amazing. Such pride. I thought they were all amazing! Dedication. So strong in the identity' (Robertson, 2006:15).

The social cohesiveness in the complementary schools was strengthened by the school activities which celebrated children's achievements in the form of regular school assemblies and end of year prizegiving ceremonies. The pupils' pride about their multiculturalism was reinforced though such celebrations. What was particularly striking in the findings in the Turkish complementary schools was how teachers valued the variations in children's accents and language use. Children were encouraged to see these variations as ways of communicating 'in different contexts (eg home versus school, talking to peers versus talking to adults)' (Creese *et al*, 2007:6). With this in mind, the same study explores how teachers allow children to negotiate learning through the use of their own variations of Turkish, while stressing the need to learn the standard form. Children's ability to code-switch between Turkish – the variation here being Cypriot Turkish – and English was seen as 'natural unmarked choice' (*ibid*, p8). Such experiences were seen as important components in the development of children's multilingual identities.

Both reports noted that classroom practices contributed to the teaching and learning of the standard forms of language and the expectation that children were to be literate in them. The content of teaching reflected the culture and history of the countries of origin, focusing on national days and other celebrations.

Following an invitation by the management committee of the East London Turkish School mentioned by Creese *et al*, two lecturers at the London Metropolitan University paid it several visits. The summary report is published here with the permission of the school and can be found on page 26.

Structure and management of complementary schools

Complementary schools were set up by members of the communities to cater for what they perceived to be lacking in the mainstream school system. In the case of migrant communities it was for the purpose of maintaining the language and customs of the country of origin. The African Caribbean schools were mainly concerned with the lack of educational opportunities for their children in mainstream schools.

Schools in our project are generally managed by elected management groups. These are made up of parents who are nominated and elected by the parents each year. The schools we visited held weekly meetings at the end of the school day, some time between noon and late afternoon, depending on the activities of the schools. Meetings were often chaired by the member of the committee elected as head of the school. General concerns of the whole school were discussed by the staff and the executive committee of the school. These might include issues with parents and the day to day matters such as lateness to school, discipline, planning and teaching and organisation of events. Some issues evoked disagreement, causing lengthy debates between the staff and the management groups and raised voices might sometimes be heard. In one such meeting one of the authors, invited as a consultant to report on a training programme, witnessed a debate precipitated by a teacher who expressed his concern about the chair's 'manner' in addressing his staff, and this escalated into an argument.

The heads of the schools also organise and chair meetings with parents. They often try to act as a go-between for all parties on issues concerning parents and teachers. One of the most frequent areas of contention relates to parental expectations of how children should be treated. Heated debates arise between teachers and parents.

Some language schools are supported by teachers from overseas who are employed by the Embassies. Although there have been some improvements through training, the expectations of some of these teachers are often in conflict with those of parents and the teachers who are trained in Britain.

In the effort to diffuse such tensions, the heads of schools arranged meetings for teachers and parents. Because the schools pay for their premises out of their own budget, there are time constraints. This means that general meetings where issues can be fully debated can only be held four or five times a year. This is also the time when the executive committee is elected. Due to the voluntary nature of all posts it is not uncommon for heads of schools to be re-elected on annual basis. One such head who is a close associate of one of the authors has expressed his dismay at his repeated attempts to resign his position, efforts which he described as being 'blocked' by his own staff, who did not want him to leave.

The content, styles of teaching and the curriculum

Apart from the *Quality Framework* developed by the NRC to help complementary schools to improve services (see page 17) there are no centrally organised systems to help complementary schools to regulate their provision.

Schools act as independent forums to deliver the curriculum they see as best fulfilling their ethos. For language schools the main focus is to teach the language, history and customs of the country of origin. For African Caribbean schools it is often the National Curriculum materials used in mainstream UK schools plus materials used for religious instruction.

In most language schools materials are imported from the country of origin.Often they are heavily nationalistic and have no real relevance to children's experiences as bilinguals growing up in the UK. Sadly this is sometimes reflected in the attitudes of certain teachers who are unfamiliar with the children's experiences. In one school we visited, we saw a Turkish teacher reprimand a pupil for his 'ignorance' about Turkish history. However it is fair to say that such attitudes are slowly changing. A good deal of positive practice by both Embassy teachers as well as those directly employed by the schools was apparent. In our 'evaluative' visit to a Turkish Community School in East London we noted the strengths of this school below – but also the areas which needed development.

Strengths

- the relationships with the pupils were positive
- the teaching was enthusiastic and most tasks set were appropriate to the pupils' levels
- the resources used in some classes were very imaginative
- in some classes pupils were given individual support
- the level of subject knowledge across the school was high.

Areas for development

- in some classes there should be less emphasis on whole class teaching and more on differentiated group activities. This will allow teachers to plan more appropriately for individual support
- to maximise pupils' understanding, more time could be given to modelling and explaining major tasks
- teachers could try to strike a greater balance between their talk time and that of the pupils. This should help pupils' confidence in using Turkish.
- sufficient time should be allocated to round things off at the end of lessons.

Alison Hatt and Tözün Issa, February 2007

A survey on complementary schools in Leicester (Martin *et al*, 2004) illustrated how 'bilingualism and bilingual teaching/learning is managed'. They mention teachers urging students to speak Gujarati while managing a skilful juxtaposition of English' (2004:13). Similar findings were confirmed in a recent study on two Turkish complementary schools in London, where teachers focused on the significance of Standard Turkish while not totally discouraging children from speaking English in class (Creese, 2007:4). It was also revealed in both studies that teachers adopted a broad perspective to language teaching. Although some teachers had poor English language skills, they appeared to be willing to learn the meaning of certain English words from their pupils. This 'appeared to widen participants' choice' resulting in higher levels of interaction between teachers and pupils (Creese *et al*, 2007:6) while helping to 'maintain their identities', so adding to classroom cohesion (Martin *et al*, 2004:16). A particularly striking finding relating at the Turkish schools is the way children's code-switching helped their use of 'full linguistic repertoires to learn and play' (Creese *et al*, 2007:8).

Teaching is hampered by the shortage of time for lesson preparation rather than the inability of teachers to appreciate interactive teaching approaches. Almost all the teachers interviewed for the present study have indicated that children would definitely benefit from child centred approaches. They identified time as the biggest constraint on their preparation.

The next three chapters offer a more comprehensive and analytical account of content, styles of teaching and the curriculum in London complementary schools.

PART TWO
The London Complementary Schools Project

3

Research methodology and categorisation of schools

Our key objective in this study was to investigate the curriculum complementary schools offered their communities. Were they academic – related to the national curriculum – or were they cultural and religious, intent on maintaining community continuity? We identified two broad categories of complementary schools: language schools and black complementary schools. We categorised these further according to the curriculum they emphasised: community language; the national curriculum, in particular English, maths, science and ICT; Religious education and black African/ Caribbean history and Afrocentric culture. We wanted to find out whether any of the responding schools offered combinations of these elements, and if so, which.

Methodology

We carried out a large-scale survey to establish the current provision in complementary schools, through a mailed questionnaire (see Appendix) which we devised and sent to 850 schools operating mainly in London. We also sent a few to schools outside London. We used the database kept by the National Resource Centre for Supplementary Schools for our mailing.

We were interested in finding out the following information through the questionnaires:

■ how long had the school had been operating?

- ■ who taught there?
- ■ where the teachers had qualified: in their country of origin or were they British trained?
- ■ which communities did the school serve?
- ■ what type of curriculum did they offer?

Our questionnaire wanted to know:

- – the name of school or contact person
- – when and why the school was started
- – the number of teaching staff
- – the type of training or qualification undertaken by members of staff and whether additional training was provided
- – the type of curriculum offered
- – the number of children attending the school and their nationality, cultural or ethnic heritage
- – which main communities the school served

We recognised that the number of questionnaires returned might be small, as so often happens with large-scale surveys. However we chased up the questionnaires by phoning schools and making personal contact with the directors of centres and the teachers. These personal contacts increased the number of returns and in some cases facilitated our visits to a small selection of schools. However, the number of schools we managed to contact directly was affected by time and financial constraints. Of the 820 questionnaires sent out we received completed forms from 52 language schools and 18 black and African Caribbean schools.

We analysed the responses according to the issues listed above. Rather than think about possible combinations that might emerge from the subcategories (which we counted to be as high as 29), we decided to analyse the responses in order to determine the final categories. We thought of many possible combinations so we decided to wait and see what subcategories would emerge. We ended up with those shown on table 3.1.

Table 3.1 Schools with types of curriculum offered

(Percentages in brackets)							
LANGUAGE SCHOOLS (TI)							
Community Language (CL)	National Curriculum (NC)	Religious (RE)	BOTH CL&NC	BOTH RE&CL	BOTH RE&NC	THREE (Any three) categories	FOUR (All four categories)
22 (42.3%)	2 (3.9%)	-	11 (21.1%)	8 (15.4%)	-	8 (15.4%)	1 (1.9%)

Nearly 42.5 per cent of the language schools that responded to the questionnaires indicated that they catered for community language instruction. A total of eighteen different languages were offered: Turkish, Arabic, Gujarati, French, Spanish, Tamil, Croatian, Farsi, Urdu, Korean, Somali, Hungarian, Bengali, Kurdish, Greek, Russian, Finnish and Mandarin.

Just over 21 per cent indicated that they offered both community languages and national curriculum support in English, maths and science. One school offered ICT only, while another offered support in English alongside the community language. Fifteen point four per cent of schools indicated that they offered community language along with Religious Education. These schools were shown as Catholic, Islamic (Koranic), Hindu and Sikh.

The combination in subcategories varied. Nearly 15.5 per cent of all the responding schools offered instruction in three combination subcategories: 80 per cent (ie 8) indicated that they offered Community Language (HL), national curriculum (NC) and Religious Education (RE) while 20 per cent (ie two), showed a combination of CL, RE and Afro-centric curriculum (AFC) subcategories, indicating that they taught African Caribbean Culture and History.

Only 3.9 per cent (2 out of 52) of schools offered support in NC only. The subjects were English, maths and science. One school (1.9%) offered a curriculum in all four categories, and none offered Religious Education alone. Neither did any school offer NC and RE together.

Further examination of the categories revealed the diversity and complexity of complementary schools. The types of curriculum provided showed that community language provision was offered to over 500 children within this small sample.

We now look at each of the subcategories in detail.

Types of curriculum offered

Subcategory 1: community language instruction

The community language instruction group formed the biggest subcategory, with 23 schools (42.4%) of the 52 responding schools. The statistical information relating to these schools is listed in Table 3.2 below.

Most schools operated at weekends with some running on weekday evenings. One school that had operated for ten years offered classes on both Sunday and Saturday.

The list of schools demonstrates the variation in size and the number of students they accommodate. The smallest school catered for twelve children and the largest for 290.

The number of children in the school determines the number of teaching and non-teaching staff. There are relatively few UK trained teachers in the language instruction schools, compared to those trained from abroad. This need not be a problem but it does suggest that the teachers require training to acquire the skills to teach children who are born in the UK.

A large number of schools are well established. Q, a Greek school, was set up in 1966, and more than fifteen others have been in operation for over ten years.

The most recent, H, is a Latin American school which has run for two years. How long a school has been operating gives some indication of the length of time the community has been established in England. Demographic changes in some areas of London, as well as social mobility in certain communities may result in new community schools being established in different areas. For example, the first Turkish complementary school was established in Soho in central London in 1962, to serve communities all around London. Later, schools were established

Table 3.2: The Language Schools in the London Complementary Schools Project

Name of School	Teaching staff	Volunteers	Overseas Trained	UK Qualified	Children M/F (Total)	Age Range	Community Group/s it serves	Day/s	How many years as a school
A	6	3	6	6	30/60 (90)	10-16	Somali	Sat & Sun	10
B	15	18	10	5	98/111 (209)	5-18	Turkish	Sat	13
C	13	12	13	5	141/127 (268)	5-13	Iraqi	Sat	4
D	9	16	9	-	52/65 (117)	5-18	Turkish	Sat	20
E	7	4	2	-	25/65 (90)	2-16	Gujerati	Sat	25
F	5	-	2	2	23/27 (50)	3-14	French/British Iranian, Mauritian	Sat	5
G	1	-	1	-	8/9 (17)	5-11	Turkish	Sat	5
H	2	1	1	-	8/8 (16)	6-12	Latin American	Sat	2
I	7	7	3	4	82/80 (162)	5-17	Indian, Sri-Lankan	Sat	17
J	1	1	1	1	3/13 (16)	4-12	Croatian	Sat	11
K	9	11	6	4	25/20 (45)	3-19	Iranian/Afghani	Sat	17
L	4	6	3	3	14/34 (48)	7-20	Urdu speaking	Sat	5

Table 3.2: The Language Schools in the London Complementary Schools Project continued

Name of School	Teaching staff	Volunteers	Overseas Trained	UK Qualified	Children M/F (Total)	Age Range	Community Group/s it serves	Day/s	How many years as a school
M	3	3	3	1	6/6 (12)	4-11	Korean (N.Ireland)	Sat	12
N	8	8	15	1	26/23 (49)	1-16	Hungarian	Sat	18
O	3	2	3	1	21/20 (41)	5-15	Bangladeshi	Mon-Thur.	12
P	3	3	3	-	14/10 (24)	5-16	Kurdish	Sat.	17
Q	11	5	10	-	(178)	4-18	Greek	Sat.	41
R	27	34	34	4	NA		Russian	NA	4
S	13	18	18	NA	(100)	1-16	Finnish	Sat.	21
T	10	10	6	4	50/50 (100)	6-16	Gujerati	Tues	18
U	25	1	NA	NA	140/150 (290)	5-18	Iranian Afghan Tajik	Sat	24
V	5	5	4	3	18/15 (33)	5-16	Somali	Mon-Thr.	3
W	50	10	49	1	(500)	5-18	Gujarati	Sat	18

* NA not available

Table 3.3: Schools Offering National Curriculum Only

Name of School	Teaching staff	Volunteers	Overseas Trained	UK Trained with QTS	Children M/F (Total)	Age Range	Community Group/s served	Day/s Nat Cur (M/Sc/ Eng)	How many years as a school
A	6	3	6	4	30/60 (90)	10-16	Somali	M/Sc/Eng Sat/ Sun	12
B	5	3	4	3	18/15 (33)	5-16	Somali	Mon -Th. M/Sc/ Eng	4

in North London to serve more local needs and more recently schools have been set up in Shoreditch and Hackney and in South London.

Subcategory 2: National Curriculum only

Only two schools indicated that they offered NC support only (see Table 3.3). It is interesting that both schools serve the growing Somali community in London. There is more information on one of the schools in the next section.

Subcategory 3: Community Language and the National Curriculum

The schools in this category offer support to children in National Curriculum subjects, in addition to community language teaching. The majority of schools offer support in maths, science and English, as shown (see Table 3.4).

Some of the schools in this category are well-established community institutions and focus mainly on the three core National Curriculum subjects, along with the community language. Most of them operate at weekends. One noticeable aspect of the schools in this category is that their size responds to demand. One of the reasons for their popularity appeared to be the sizeable community the schools served within their vicinity. In some cases the communities they intend to serve establish the schools at locations which are easily reached. The Turkish in Hornsey, Bangladeshi schools in Whitechapel and Kurdish schools in Dalston, East London are all easily accessed by their communities. The other attraction can be explained in terms of offering more options for the parents. National Curriculum (NC) support appears to attract more pupils, as can been seen in school G (Turkish) in Table 3.5. The school focus on curriculum support has also attracted attendance from monolingual English children.

Subcategory 4: Community language teaching and Religious Education

This group includes some from outside London eg Leicester, where there is a sizeable established minority community. Most of these schools have been functioning for a long time, teaching first and second generation bilinguals. This appears to support our finding that Religious Education is regarded as an important aspect of complementary education and seen as contributing to and maintaining community cohesion. This category also shows that community language instruction is not seen as incompatible with religious instruction.

Table 3.4: Community Language plus National Curriculum

Name of School	Teaching staff	Volunteers	Overseas Trained	UK Trained with QTS	Children M/F (Total)	Age Range	Community Group/s served	Day/s Nat Cur (M/Sc/Eng)	How many years as a school
A	8	3	9	2	50/60 (110)	8-17	Moroccan	Sat M/Sc/Eng.	15
B	10	3	6	4	80/60 (140)	5-16	Bangladeshi	Sat M/Sc/Eng.	30
C	4	-	4	-	25/25 (50)	3-14	French British Iranian Algerian	M/Sc Eng.	15
D	4	4	2	2	32/20 (52)	8-16	Kurdish Turkish	Sat M/Sc/Eng	6
E	12	8	12	-	40/60 (100)	3-16	Latin American	Sat M/Sc/Eng.\	6
F	10	4	14	1	NA	2.5-19	Georgian	Sat IT/History	5

Table 3.4: Community Language plus National Curriculum continued

Name of School	Teaching staff	Volunteers	Overseas Trained	UK Trained with QTS	Children M/F (Total)	Age Range	Community Group/s served	Day/s Nat Cur (M/Sc/ Eng)	How many years as a school
G	16	8	5	8	90/120 (210)	4-16	Turkish	Sat M/Sc/ Eng.	17
H	17	11	12	5	27/35 (62)	6-14	Turkish English	Sat M/Sc/ Eng.	4
I	5	8	2	3	72/58 (130)	6-11	Turkish / Kurdish	Sat M/Sc/ Eng.	2
J	4	-	2	1	11/7 (18)	2-5	Chinese	Sat M/Sc/ Eng.	21
L						5-16	Turkish	Sat M/Sc/ Eng.	4
M	1	2	-	1	10/10 (20)	2-11	French	Sat M/Sc/ Eng.	25
O	5	1	4	1	54/56 (110)	5-11	Iranian	Sat Eng	22

Table 3.5: Community Language and Religious Education

Name of School	Teaching staff	Volunteers	Overseas Trained	UK Trained with QTS	Children M/F (Total)	Age Range	Community Group served	Day/s Rel-gious Inst.	How many years as a school
A	12	-	12	-	150/150 (300)	6-18	Panjabi	Tue-Fri Sun **Sikhism**	19
B	2	1	2	-	14/21 (35)	6-18	Panjabi	Sun **Sikhism**	12
C	27	5	25	1	150/200 (350)	5.5-15	Gujarati (Leicester)	NA **Hinduism**	40
D	2	2	-	1	6/3 (9)	5-11	Ukrainian (Leicester)	Ukrainian Orthodox	30
E	2	2	2	-	20/25 (45)	7-16	Panjabi	Th/Fri **Sikhism**	20
F	14	17	14	6	82/78 (160)	3.5-12	Arab	Sat **Islam**	25
G	5	3	5	-	-	5-14	Polish	Mon/Wed **Catholic**	50
H	22	22	18	3	56/44 (100)	7-18	Hindu	Sat **Hindu**	20

Our overall findings suggest that complementary schools have moved away from their initial traditional role of instruction in community language to develop a multiplicity of functions. This can partly be explained as a response to parental choice as well as the demands of the NC. Statistically some communities still underperform in national curriculum subjects. The role of complementary schools is seen partly as offering support in the NC. As shown by the examples in Category 3 (above) and categories 5 and 6 (below), many schools have responded to the wider issues of underachievement of some ethnic groups in mainstream schools and pressure from a majority of parents who want to see their children learning a community language and enhancing some of their learning in mainstream school.

Subcategory 5: Schools offering three types of curriculum
Schools in this section reflected three of the four categories listed in Table 3.1: CL, NC, RE *or* Afrocentric curriculum (AC) (see Table 3.6). This section is comparatively small, but it appears to represent a cross-section of complementary schools offering three types of curriculum.

We can assume that offering all three types of curriculum is becoming more widespread across the various community groups. This strengthens our argument that complementary schools are moving away from the traditional teaching of community language only to also supporting pupils' learning of both the NC and cultural topics.

More importantly, the role of complementary schools is seen by providers and parents as an extension of similar learning in mainstream schools. This category signals the changing perception of complementary schools as being single category institutions that offer one form of learning only.

Subcategory 6: Schools offering four types of curriculum
Only one school offered all four types of curriculum (see Table 3.7). Significantly, this school was only set up in 2005, to serve the Cabindan-Angolan and Congolese communities. It is a small school, with only two qualified teachers from the UK and five with qualifications from overseas. The languages offered are French, Lingala and Kikongo and the NC subjects are English, maths and science. Religious instruction was in Christianity. The Afrocentric focus linked to the countries' past history, their African heritage, slavery and the current political situation in Cabinda and Republic of Congo.

Table 3.6: Community Language, National Curriculum and Religious Education

Name of School	Teaching staff	Volunteers	Overseas Trained	UK Trained with QTS	Children M/F (Total)	Age Range	Community Groups served	DAYS Type/s of curriculum CL/NC/RE AF-Cent. (Afro-Cent.)	How many years as a school
A	19	Yes-NA	15	-	NA	NA	NA	Sat CL/NC.RE	9
B	10	8	6	4	40/40 (80)	2-16	Asian Panjabi	Weekend CL/NC/RE	26
C	6	6	-	5	8/15 (23)	5-16	Somali	Weekend CL/NC/ AF-Cent.	12
D	4	2	2	2	20/20 (40)	8-16	Bangladeshi	Sat/Sun HL/NC/RE	7
E	27	32	-	5	65/95	5-19	Gujarati Tamil	Sat/Thr HL/NC/RE	11
F	7	8	NA	NA	70/80 (150)	5-19	Asian	Wkend CL/NC/RE	25
G	NA	NA	NA	NA	34/37 71	5-14	Turkish British	Weekends CL/NC/RE	5
H	11	1	8	NA	NA	NA	Muslim (Birmingham)	Mon-Fri CL/NC/RE	27

Table 3.7: Schools offering all four types of curriculum

Name of School	Teaching staff	Volunteers	Overseas Trained	UK Trained with QTS	Children M/F (Total)	Age Range	Community Groups served	DAYS	How many years as a school
A	7	3	5	2	5/10 (15)	11-16	Cabindan Angolan Congolese	Weekends	2

Having looked at categories of schools and types of curricula offered we now turn to our findings from visits to some of our project schools. We present these as case studies in the next chapter.

4

The London Language Schools

The case studies analyse one school from each of the subcategories identified in the last chapter. On the initial questionnaire all schools were asked to indicate whether they would welcome a follow-up visit and interview. We selected a school from each of our categories accordingly and arranged a convenient time to visit. Twenty five schools responded to the questionnaire but three were incomplete. Pursuing the schools with phone calls yielded four more. An agreed set of questions was devised for us to ask all participants.

Sample lessons were observed and children, teachers, volunteers workers, parents and school directors or leaders were interviewed. We made a total of twelve visits, two per subcategory, and spent 36 hours collecting data. We wanted to see how the languages were taught and learned, the amount of preparation by teachers and the engagement of the pupils.

Case study 1: Anatolian Turkish School: School L (Category 3; community language and national curriculum combined)

The school is situated in the London borough of Haringey. It uses the premises of a local secondary school but not the facilities. During our visit we saw several parent volunteers helping with various activities in the school. This included setting up stalls for food and drink, helping teachers to guide children to their classes and helping with classroom support.

We observed a language session led by a student teacher who was completing her final PGCE practice as part of her school placement for complementary schools. The class consisted of a mixed group of sixteen children ages 11 and 12, in years 6 and 7. A summary of the lesson and evaluation is presented below.

Lesson Observation 1

The objective of the lesson was *to learn adjectives that describe animals in Turkish*.

The teacher's lesson plan was clear and laid out step by step procedures for achieving the learning objective. Mrs. Gökce first re-established the ground rules for the lesson and reminded the class of her expectations of their behaviour during the lesson. She then explained the learning objective to the class and moved to asking questions about each of the animal pictures she had placed on the board.

> *Bu hayvanın adı ne?* (What is the name of this animal?)
>
> *Saçları ne renk bu atın?* (What colour is this horse's hair?)
>
> *Atı bana tarif edin desem neler söylersiniz?* (If I ask you to describe the horse, what would you say about it?)

Key adjectives were written on the board and the children were encouraged to look at them. Mrs. Gökce used the Turkish adjectives each time she asked children to think about a word to describe the horse. She carefully wrote these down on the board, giving the children good models and guidance for forming their own sentences. The relevant sentences were placed underneath pictures.

The language and questions were carefully planned and the children were asked to think about the language tasks in stages of complexity in seeking information. The questions served this purpose very well.

The lesson continued with the children working in small groups with different packs of pictures of various animals and listed adjectives in both English and Turkish. They were asked to choose adjectives to describe their animals.

Mrs. Gökce and the volunteers moved around the room and helped the children to recognise and match English adjectives with Turkish ones before they went on to make a sentence describing their animal.

The teacher provided plenty of visual support. The children had help with the task and responded appropriately. The animal names and adjectives were written on different coloured cards, with additional animal pictures and blank cards ready for new adjectives. She made sure that everyone was involved in the lesson. Parents were strategically placed next to challenging children and helped and supported them with their answers.

The teacher stopped and clarified teaching points whenever the need arose. The key to the success of her lesson was her use of both Turkish and English in the one lesson. This, as she explained to us, gave children the chance to link the English words with new Turkish ones and this was confirmed when we interviewed the children after the lesson. She admitted to being 'quite tired' at the end of the lesson.

The lesson ended with Mrs. Gökce asking each group to share their sentences, describing their animals with their chosen adjectives.

Observer	(to children)	Nasıl gidiyor?	How is it going?
Ali		Iyidir. Hayvanları anlatıyoruz	It's good. We are describing the animals
Observer		Önce aramızda hayvanları konuşuyoruz ve neyini yazacaksak onun Türkcesini buluyoruz aramızda konuşarak.	First we talk about the animals and decide what we are going to write about and we find out how to say it in Turkish by talking about it.
		Güzel. Şimdi ne üzerinde konuşuyorsunuz mesala?	Good. What are you working on now?
		Köpek. Bu Sivas Kangalı. Bu köpekler çok kuvvetlidir. Onun için ona kuvvetli 'köpek dedik'	A dog. This is Kangal from Sivas (Turkey). It a very strong dog so we said 'strong dog'

Observer		Peki Türkcesini bilmediğiniz bir sıfat olursa ne yaparsınız?	Ok. What happens if you don't know the Turkish for an adjective?
Ayşe		Genelde grup olarak calıştığımız için buluyoruz. Ama zor bir kelime olursa sözlükten, öğretmenden veya diğer büyüklerden. bazen de ödev olarak evde internetten bulabiliriz.	We mainly work in groups so we often find the right word. If not, we can ask our teacher or other adults here. We can use the dictionary or sometimes take things home and find out from the internet.
Observer		Kangalınızı anlatacak başka ne gibi sıfatlara bakıyorsunuz?	What else are you looking to find out about your kangal?
Elif		Mesela onun için 'Biraz vahşi' ama 'sadık' kelimelerini düşündük.	For example we have thought of 'a bit wild' and 'faithful' to describe him.
		Enteresan. Niye hem biraz vahşi hem de sadık.	Interesting. Why a bit wild as well as faithful then?
Cenk		Çünkü o kötüleri korkutur ama ayni zamanda da sahibisine çok sadıktır. Yediği yemeğe ihanet etmez.	Because he scares off the bad guys but he is also faithful to his owner. He never turns his back on the person that gives him food.
Observer		What do you like about your Saturday school?	

Ahmet			It' s fun. It makes me feel special because we can use Turkish and English. That's cool!

During the lesson we had the chance to walk around the classroom and chat to the children about their views about it. As the lesson was in Turkish we thought it appropriate to speak Turkish.

Interviews at the school

Headteachers

Q1 What do you think the school is doing well? What are the strengths of your school?

We are doing especially well with family support and student monitoring.

Q2 What are the key issues for you as a manager?

Discipline in classrooms, monitoring students' progress, relationships with certain parents and monitoring the effectiveness of our teachers.

Q3 What would help you resolve these issues?

We need more volunteers, more resources and more Government support. For example we need free access to places such as cinemas and sport centres. We also need free travel cards for our staff and students.

Q4 Anything else you want to mention about your school?

We run language classes for our parents, so when their children are in classes they are also learning. They are very happy with this.

Teachers

Q1 What do you think are the strengths of your school? What do you think the school is doing well?

I think our school is an important bridge between the Turkish speaking community and the mainstream [English speaking] culture as we try and link the positive aspects of both worlds in our work here. We also teach children to be proud of their identities while learning to respect other cultures.

We do National Curriculum booster classes in foundation subjects (years 7, 8, 9 and GCSE) here, which helps our children with their mainstream school work. For example we held a Science fair this year.

Q2 What do you like most about teaching in this school?

You can form one to one relationships with your students without damaging your role as a teacher. You become their friend as well their teacher. Some trust you to the extent of confiding in you. This is very rewarding to me as a teacher.

Q3 What are the issues for you as a teacher?
We need more volunteers to help us with our work here. [We need] support from ITT Institutions to train these people for this specialised role in community schools.

Q4 What sort of support do you need to improve your services to the community?
We urgently need funding from local authorities to buy more resources and to pay our teachers who work as volunteers or for very little money. Government should have incentives for people who may want to be trained as teachers in complementary schools.

Q5 Anything else you would like to mention relating to your role as a teacher?
Thank you for giving us the opportunity to raise some of our concerns, as well as highlighting some of the good practice which is going on in our schools. We need to work very closely with mainstream schools and train our teachers but there is no coherent strategy to facilitate this. All that seems to be happening is that authorities are paying lip service to their supposed support for complementary schools.

Parents
Q1 What do you think are the strengths of this school? What do you think the school is doing well?
Our children are learning about their culture as well as getting help with their work from full-time school.

Q2 What do you think the issues are for this school that affect you as a parent?
There are no facilities for our children to use here. For example we have no access to computers. Also some teachers from overseas do not have a real understanding of the system here so their approach to teaching is different from those who are trained in the UK.

Q3 How do you think the situation might be improved?
We need more qualified teachers as well as funding for training and resources so that what my son gets here is more in line with what he is getting in his full-time school.

Children

Q1 What do you like most about your school?

I learn Turkish, which helps me to speak to my parents and grandparents and the community. I also use it when I go on holiday in Turkey.

We do some work which is the same as in my other [mainstream] school except it is in Turkish. It helps me to understand it better and my Turkish gets better. It's fun!

Q2 What do you like least about your school?

Wish it wasn't on Saturdays. I get tired sometimes.

Q3 Do you think what you learn here helps you with your learning in your English school?

Definitely. For example we were doing some science work on metals and their properties last week. We had the same lesson in my English school last month. We did this in Turkish and English here. That means it was a good revision for me. It was also fun to learn that names of some metals were almost identical in Turkish and English.

Q4 Is there anything you want to say about your Saturday school?

This school teaches me how to be proud of being Turkish as well as British. I have the best of both worlds. It can't be bad!

Case Study 2: Bonjour! French Saturday School: School F, Category 1 (community language instruction)

Bonjour has been serving a French speaking community in North London comprising Iranian, Mauritian, British and French people, since 1991. It is a small school with 50 children and five teaching staff as well as a number of volunteers helping in the classrooms. All the staff have qualifications, some from the UK as well as overseas.

Lesson observation

The lesson observed was of a junior class, with children aged 7 and 8. The class had twelve students who were described by their teacher Miss Bellion as achieving 'stage 2 French speakers', which meant they were able to communicate and understand classroom instructions in French and could read and write basic French.

The Learning objective for this class was to *tell the time on an analogue and a digital clock.*

Miss Bellion was trained in the UK and was in her second year of teaching. She taught in a mainstream primary school and was a native French speaker.

She introduced the learning objectives and explained clearly what they were going to do that morning. She spent a couple of minutes with each student, asking them about their plans for the weekend and about their work in their full time school. It was good to see her using two languages and encouraging children to use correct French by rephrasing their sentences. She was very receptive to those who preferred to respond in English. She established rapport with her students from the beginning and this contributed to the pleasant atmosphere in the classroom.

Miss Bellion started her lesson by putting a large clock on the board and asking children to name features of the clock in French, for example the French for clock, time, big hand, small hand. She then modelled 6 o'clock, and asked if anyone could tell her in English what time it was. Everyone put their hands up. She then asked if anyone could tell her the same time in French. She helped the children by giving clues in French.

Miss Bellion repeated the same question, showing different times on the clock. She prepared flashcards with various times written in French. She placed these next to smaller clocks with similar times shown on them. The challenge was to match the writing to the clock showing that time. This made the task accessible for the children who needed additional support to make the link with the clock time and the writing that represented it. A digital clock displaying 6 o'clock was introduced and the children's responses elicited. The children responded simultaneously. A similar process was repeated as if with analogue clocks.

The children were put into ability groups and, with prepared resources, were expected to match pictures on the digital clocks to the actual time written. They then had to show the time on their cardboard clocks. Miss Bellion explained the tasks in French and English. She used mainly French but supported it with English. We (the observers) were shown different times on the clocks and were taught how to say the time in French.

This was a happy learning environment. Miss Bellion's calm and softly spoken manner had a good effect, encouraging the children to work

Observer 1		Bonjour! What time is that on the board?	
Dominic		Bonjour! It's five o'clock	
Observer 1		Yes! It's good, well done! How would you say 5.30 in French?	
Dominic		*Il est cinq heures et demie.*	It's five o'clock
Observer 1	repeats	*Il est cinq heures et demie*	
Observer 2	To another child	And how would you say 4.30?	
Josette		*Quatre heures et demie*	
Observer 2	(repeats)	*Quatre heures et demie*	
Observer 1		Do you speak French at home?	
Josette		Yes. We speak French as well but mostly English	
Observer 1		Did you know how to tell the time in French?	
David		Some of the easy ones. Here Miss Bellion says it in English first then we can learn how to say it in French. When we get it right she tells us we are clever!	

industriously. The next extract records a group of children working together to match the times on the clocks.

In the next extract a group of children are working together to match the times on the clocks.

Alex	(showing a clock with a different time) showing seven thirty	*Non, il n'est pas six heures at demie. C'est ceci, regardez!* *Il est sept heures et demie.*	No! it's not six thirty. It's this one look! It's seven thirty!
Cecile	Looking at the other clock Taking another clock	*D'accord. J'ai pensé qu'il était six heures.* *Et alors, ceci? Je sais, je sais! Ne me le dites pas! Il est sept heures quinze.*	Alright. I thought it was six What's this one then? I know, I know! Don't tell me. It's seven fifteen
Alex		Yes. Yes	
Dominique	Giving a puzzled look at the digital clock	Hey! What do you think this is?	
Alex		*Il est cinq heures quarante-cinq*	It's five forty five
Adam	Objecting	*Non. Il est six heures moins le quart.*	No. It's quarter to six
Dominique		*Ça veut dire la même chose!*	Both are the same thing!
Miss Bellion	comes to the table		How are we doing here?

The plenary was lively. All the children showed their cardboard clocks. It was clear that the learning objectives were achieved; the dual language lesson was well received and understood. Miss Bellion used the plenary as an opportunity to extend learning to quarter past and half past. With the confidence gained from the previous task, the children demonstrated their understanding by readily linking their learning to the new task.

The teacher spotted some children who looked a little unsure and she took the opportunity to note this and make arrangements to support them during the next session. She explained after the lesson that these children were to have extra support the following week and take home sample exercises to do with their parents.

Interviews at Bonjour School

Questions

A Headteacher

Q1 What do you think the school is doing well? What are the strengths of your school?

We are providing a good education in French to French speaking children in London. We have a cohesive unit where everyone works to support children in their learning.

Q2 What are the key issues for you as a manager?

We need premises to expand to carry out our work more effectively. At the moment we are renting these few rooms.

Q3 What would help you resolve these issues?

We need more resources and more support from our government as well as the local authorities.

Q4 Anything else you want to mention about your school?

Our school plays an important role in socialising bilingual children in the context of the complexities of a multicultural city. I feel that due to the demands of the National Curriculum, this appears to be lacking in most mainstream schools. We therefore need less talk and more support from the Government.

Teachers

Q1 What do you think are the strengths of your school? What do you think the school is doing well?

I think we are proving a good education in French language and culture. Most of our children study French as a foreign language in their other schools. What we do here enhances their learning further.

Q2 What do you like most about teaching in this school?

I see the children who come here as my own. We are a small and happy family here. You can afford to treat children as individuals, which helps to form strong bonds with your students. This is a very important aspect of learning in my view.

Q3 What are the issues for you as a teacher?

We need proper classrooms with resources to help us teach better. There is nothing here. We have to prepare and bring everything from outside.

Q4 What sort of support do you need to improve the services you provide to the community?

We urgently need funding from the LEA to buy more resources for our school. We urgently need classroom resources such as card, paper as well as materials to make colourful artwork and displays. We also need access to computers.

Q5 Anything else you would like to mention relating to your role as a teacher?
We are all volunteers here which means we are doing this out of the good-ness of our hearts. We do not want gold medals. We simply want our impor-tant work to be appreciated by the Government.

Parents

Q1 What do you think are the strengths of this school? What do you think the school is doing well?
Our children are learning about their culture as well as getting help with their work for their mainstream school. Due to the size and the ethos of our school each child benefits from our individualised support and 'family like' [parent's emphasis] *approach.*

Q2 What do you think are the issues for this school that affect you as a parent?
I think the school could do with more resources and having its own premises. For example our children have no access to computers here.

Q3 How do you think matters could be improved?
This is definitely a funding issue. Our LEA does not seem to think that we are making a useful contribution here. They [LA] do what they like because it is the government they see as their model.

D Children

Q1 What do you like most about your school?
My French has definitely become better since I joined the school. You also learn some of the things you do in your other school. Everyone is friendly. You can talk to anybody. It's fun being here.

Q2 What do you like least about your school?
I wish we had a place to play during break times.

Q3 Do you think what you learn here helps you with your learning in your English school?
Yes, all the time. If I learn something new in French I ask the teacher what that is in English and when she tells me I remember it in French. Using two lan-guages is very good. My teacher makes me feel important because I speak two languages. I guess she is right, I am special in this way.

Q4 Is there anything you want to say about your Saturday school?
This school is fun. I feel like this is my big family. It's different from my other school. Teachers don't have much time to talk to you there. Most of the time they do that when they are telling you off. I like my Saturday school.

5

The African Caribbean and African Schools

Eighteen schools responded to the survey and a number of schools known to us were pursued with follow up phone calls and visits. These resulted in additional schools completing and returning their questionnaire. But they appeared more receptive to face to face contact and indicated that they welcomed a visit from us, attaching names and contact number to their questionnaires. One school stated that they would only be prepared to answer our questionnaire and interview questions by post, but were too busy to accommodate a face to face follow up interview.

The statistical responses to cold postal questionnaires have already been reported. However for the African Caribbean complementary schools, responding outright to questionnaires was not a priority. 'There is nothing to be gained by schools managing on volunteer goodwill and very limited financial resources responding to an unknown request', as one school told us. We believe that call-backs regarding questionnaires were carried out by colleagues who were also part of the complementary schools network and that these increased the number of responses of African Caribbean schools in the London area. One school outside London also responded. Our personal contacts and networking lead us to believe we could have increased our return numbers but time and finances imposed limitations.

In the 1970s and 1980s complementary schools tried to correct the discriminatory and inadequate general education received by black children. Saturday schools, as they were generally known, concentrated on teaching reading, writing, mathematics, history and geography. The history and geography syllabus focused on teaching about Africa's ancient civilisations, the trans-Atlantic slave trade, the Americas and the Caribbean, and the establishment of colonial and neocolonial relationships with Britain and Europe that shaped our lives and our relationship with Europe (Fryer, 1984). The need to counter the racism of the curriculum, that undermined and destroyed many black children's motivation and self-esteem, was and remains a determining factor in the construction of the Afrocentric curriculum. This curriculum positions the African diaspora, history, cultures and achievements as crucial and relevant to motivating and inspiring black children to re-engage with learning, learning focused on academic attainment as well as the personal and emotional development of children and their parents.

We used Afrocentric as one of the categories to classify the data schools used to describe African Caribbean methodology. This was reflected in the schools' ethos, curriculum, teaching materials and resources, including personnel. The other three categories are: the English national curriculum including ICT, and those that had either a religious or heritage language pedagogy. Pseudonyms were used to preserve the identity of the Black schools. Where additional information is known either from visits made or additional documentation received from the schools, it is noted in the columns.

The schools were categorised by the provision they offered (see Chapter 3) but in all cases the emphasis on an Afrocentric (AC) curriculum was a strong feature and for thirteen it was particularly dominant and explicit. Even where the curriculum did not explicitly teach African Caribbean history, the environment and prevailing attitudes and ethos of the school personnel exalted success, black pride, and achievement as part of its culture and its reason for being in existence. This was apparent in the comments made on the questionnaires and the accompanying literature and in some cases was further confirmed during visits to the schools. Kaye's brochure states:

> People of all ages come to Kaye. They come to study core curriculum subjects and therefore to improve their academic and employment prospects. They also come to learn about and celebrate their cultural heritage.

Africa, Unity and Maroons deliberately select Afrocentric teaching resources and materials to support learning in the national curriculum and employ mother tongue to assist the children's understanding of curriculum materials .

All the Black schools offered teaching or tutorials in National Curriculum subjects, particularly in mathematics, English, science. Black history, geography and creative arts featured in the curriculum and would be demonstrated in 'graduation and social celebrations'. The older established schools and those with secure accommodation were able offer ICT access, so enabling secondary school age students to complete school projects. They also afforded access to computers.

Yam and Progressive both operated in mainstream school buildings and had mixed fortunes regarding access to resources. Yam had access to the school in which it operated and was given strong support from the school management. Some of the teachers from the main school also taught at Yam. Progressive, however, had access only to the main hall and adjacent toilets. All other resources required for the day had to be brought in, including snacks and notice boards.

Six of the more established schools which had operated for six years or more could offer sessions in the evenings as well as all day Saturday. Some, like Africa, also offered individual or group tutorial opportunities to older students in the evenings. Treasure and Maroons mentioned that in addition to their academic focus, children attended mid-week sessions that included sports, African arts and cultural activities.

No school offered Religious Education exclusively. Four schools, Jamo, Mandela, Roots and Unity, operated within a religious framework, one Islamic and the others Christian. Africa and Central also had a religious ethos that informed their practice and interactions with the children and the community. Religion, however, is not part of the taught curriculum or the *modus operandi* in either school. Central is housed in a community building which is also its church. Africa is funded by and

Types of curriculum offered by black complementary schools

Names	African Centric	National Curriculum	Religious Education	Mother Tongue
1 Africa	AC Demonstrated in children's presentations and celebration of achievements	NC including ICT	Founded by the church, but accessible to the local community	*languages of the children used in school, but not as language of instruction
2 Amy	AC Also empower parents to help children	NC		
3 Baddish		NC		
4 Blacks	AC African Caribbean resources used to support teaching	NC including ICT		
5 Central	AC Some black resources to support NC	NC	Religion not taught but school functions within a religious ethos	
6 Jamo	AC Included in language and AC data	NC	RE	MT (discussed in Language Schools in ch 3)
7 Kaye	AC	NC including ICT		
8 Marcus	AC	Has access to the ICT resources and facilities		

Names	African Centric	National Curriculum	Religious Education	Mother Tongue Children's mother tongue used in class, by teachers and children but not as language of instruction
9 Maroons	AC Reflected in its aims	NC		
10 Mandela	AC	NC	RE	
11 Olive	AC	NC including ICT		
12 Progressive		NC		
13 Roots		NC	RE	
14 Treasure	AC	NC including ICT		
15 Unity		NC	RE	
16 Yam	AC	NC		MT
17 Youth		NC		
18 Zenzy	AC	NC		

based in its church building. In both schools the teachers are drawn from church members, as are most of children who attend the school. However, other children from the neighbourhood also attend the school. In Africa, staff communicated with parents and children by means of their shared mother tongues. The children's heritage languages, like religion, did not form part of the curriculum and the school did not identify itself as a community language school. Africa had a friendly and welcoming atmosphere and parents were made welcome when they dropped in. They would talk to staff about their children's progress and catch up with news and information from 'back home'.

Three schools, Baddish, Progressive and Youth, indicated that they concentrated exclusively on the national curriculum. The prevailing ethos at Progressive was that every child can and will learn, achieve and become a confident and successful learner. Children's skills and successes were publicly acclaimed within the setting, shared with parents and recorded. Progress and achievements were attached to children's school work, conduct and presentation of self. Parents were consulted and given regular feedback on their child's progress. As with Africa, parents had ready access to the teachers. Progressive's positive attitudes towards the children and their learning and achievements echo features of the Afrocentric ethos of other complementary schools.

Baddish is located in an education authority, in which a disproportionately high number of black children underachieve and, like Progressive, has an ethos that is extremely positive and dedicated to supporting black children's learning. The head teacher wrote: '...the project aims to break down barriers, stimulate self esteem and enable children to achieve their optimum potential'.

Community languages in black complementary schools

Four schools actively used the children's heritage languages. Two, Maroons and Unity, used children's community languages to support their learning and would translate any difficult concept which arose in class into English. The community language was used in adult to adult interactions as well as during informal teacher-pupil interactions including spontaneous reprimands. Unity and Jamo used the community language as the mode of instruction. Unity employed Arabic in teaching religious instruction and Somali as the language in which to transmit and teach culture and customs.

Just over one thousand children in all attended the eighteen schools recorded in our data. There were slightly more girls than boys (13). The teacher-child ratio, not including volunteers, is approximately thirteen to one. Including the volunteers, the ratio of adults to children drops to about nine to one. The numbers of overseas trained teachers was relatively small, (11). One school, Yam, had five teachers who held both overseas and UK teaching qualifications. Another notable feature was the ten volunteer students working at Amy, all recruited from the local college and university.

Youth started in 2005 at the request of parents, most of whom were 'Black Africans'. It had three teachers with UK qualified teacher status and three teaching assistants with oversees degrees and was one of only four schools that had slightly more boys than girls. The school boasted a teacher student ratio of eleven to one at key stage 2 of the National Curriculum and provided tuition in literacy, numeracy and science for 30 Saturdays over the academic year. The school worked within the ethos of the local Church of England primary school and the head-teacher believes that the school can really make a difference and help the children to achieve academic success at key stage 2.

Observation of an early years group

A mixture of teaching styles was observed in the schools visited: small and large groups, whole class teaching, chalk and talk and one to one tutorials for older children.

Nine children, four girls and five boys aged 4 or 5, were observed working at a teacher directed task. Screens divided the space in the main hall, of this shop front, now a vibrant church. Two other groups of children worked in this space. One, of about twelve children, was being taught mathematics by the director of the school, while a group of five worked independently. The school is located close to a busy street market, and the school has an open door policy which operates when the school is open. Parents of the children attending the school and members of the congregation are all welcome to visit the church and the school. Another screen separates the children from the front of the

All African Caribbean Schools

Names	Teaching Staff	Volunteer	Overseas Trained	UK Qualified	Children M/F	Age Range	Community group served	Day/s operation	Years in operation
1 AFRICA	6	3		3	25F 20M	5 - 11	African Caribbean	Sat	1
2 AMY	2	10			18	5 -16+	African Caribbean	Sat	21
3 BADDISH	3	4		3	13F 19M	5-16+	African Caribbean	Sat	6
4 BLACKS	5	3	Non teaching qualifications	5	80	5-16	African Caribbean	Wed Thur, Fri & Sat	20+
5 CENTRAL	4			4	Approx 24 no. fluctuated in relation to school term	5- 11	African Caribbean	Sat	8
6 JAMO *this school appears in both Language and AC data	2	5		5	19F 5M	11-16	African Cabindan Angolan Congolese	Week ends	2

Names	Teaching Staff	Volunteer	Overseas Trained	UK Qualified	Children M/F	Age Range	Community group served	Day/s	Years in operation
7 KAYE	14	2		14	125	5-16	African, African Caribbean	Tue-Sat	20+
8 LANSDOWNE	2	2		2	9F 6M	5-16	African	Sat	5
9 MANDELA	3	2	1	3	12F 10M	5-16+	African Caribbean	Sat	12
10 MAROONS	2	3		2	24	5-16	African Caribbean	Thu, Fri, Sat	9
11 MARCUS	2	1		1	6F 7M	8-16	African African Caribbean	Sat	4
12 OLIVE	5	3	2	3	22F 19M	5-15, plus support for adult learners	African plus African Caribbean, for adult Indo-Caribbean	Sat	20+
13 PROGRESSIVE	4			4	20F 15M	5-16	Black Black Caribbean, African. Asian. White	Sat	5

Names	Teaching Staff	Volunteer	Overseas Trained	UK Qualified	Children M/F	Age Range	Community group served	Day/s	Years in operation
14 TREASURE	4	3		4	15F 21M	9-16	African	Wed, Fri & Sat	8
15 UNITY	3	3		3	10F 16M	7-16	African	Sat & Summer school	10
16 YAM	7	6	5* staff hold both overseas and UK teaching qualifications	9*	40F 30M	4-16	British- Guyanan Nigerian Sierra Leone Jamaican Grenadian Bangladeshi (it was noted that these children are British nationals)	Mon, Tues, Wed 4-8 Sat and Summer Holidays	6
17 YOUTH	3 & 3 Teacher Assistants		3	3	28F 38M	5-11	Black Africans	Sat	1
18 ZENZY	2	1			17	7 -11	African Caribbean	Sat	2

building, which looks out onto a busy street, and creates a small waiting area to the front where parents with toddlers and shopping can sit and wait.

I sat with a small group of 4 to 5 year-old children. The teacher was teaching them the alphabet: how to write the letters shapes while learning the sounds for each. For some of the youngest in the group, it worked as a mark making activity. A whiteboard was propped up at the top of a large communal table and the children arranged themselves around the table within sight of the board. Each had a notebook, paper and pencils and some crayons and felt tip pens were placed within reach on the table. The teacher sounded out each letter as she wrote it and showed the children the starting point from which to write it themselves.

The pace was slow because she needed to give some children individual attention, showing them how to make the letter patterns correctly. She wrote the letter again in some of the children's books, and held the hands of others as they tried to make the correct shapes. Pacing the session was difficult as the children had different levels of writing skill and pencil control and the teacher was insistent about correct process and uniform outcomes.

The children in the group were attentive, quiet and engaged, willing to try and follow the teacher's directions. The physical and cognitive skills they needed to complete this task successfully were demanding for some of them. They were required to look up to the board, watch and remember how the letter was being drawn, while understanding the writing conventions of moving eyes and pens from left to right, while simultaneously following the direction of the letter formation from top to bottom. They had to remember each process and then physically recreate the letter stroke by stroke on lined paper on a different surface, using a different tool, a pencil.

The teacher had to leave the board and attend to children who were having difficulty with the task, holding their hands and tracing around the letter shapes, writing the letter in their books and allowing them to copy from the one she wrote in front of them. The physical seating arrangements did not help either. The tables were too high and the chairs too low; children were not encouraged to sit on their knees to reach the table comfortably, which one child repeatedly tried to do. One creative little boy who could not reach the table comfortably became distracted and quickly devised a pencil rolling game once he discovered that the smooth surface of the table guaranteed that the pencil would roll and fall off the table and he would then have to get off his chair to retrieve it. After a few retrievals, which disturbed the boy next to him, the teacher got wise to his adventure and added another chair to his seat. Once he was elevated to the right height, she reintroduced him to the alphabet task.

The teacher's expectation of the group was that they would complete all twenty-six letters of the alphabet during the one session. When they had done so, they would identify the letters of their own names, pick them out from the list and then draw and colour their pictures. The session was initially planned for 40 minutes. The teacher's plans were ambitious and would have been better served if she had more resources. Children could have been arranged in smaller groups, working on different surfaces – the floor as well as the table – and encouraged to write the letters of the alphabet that they already knew, starting with the letters of their names. Writing or mark making with a purpose would help children to move towards conventional letter formations.

Observation of a mathematics session at Progressive

A mixed ability group of children were studying maths, using a maths work book and photocopied materials identified and prepared by the teacher. A few children had counters to help them work out the problems, while the older children worked from their text. They mostly worked in silence and when they finished their task they took it to the teacher. It was interesting that the teacher did not always wait for a child to come up to him. He called up the pupils who had completed their work to bring their books for checking, and challenged them if they had not completed what was expected of them. All the children had their work marked and commented on during the session. Some would have to return to the teacher before going home, either for follow-up work or the corrections they would be expected to do for homework.

One overseas trained maths teacher working with a GCSE group told us that the children did not do their lessons at home so were not learning as well as they should. He said he would be speaking to the parents about the children doing their homework. He felt that the inadequacy of resources affected his ability to teach effectively. He was hindered by not having access to a photocopier and needed to be given time to prepare differentiated work for the children.

In Progressive the children who had not performed as well as expected or who encountered difficulties with the work were given one to one tutorials with the senior teacher, either during the session or as the parents arrived. I was told that parents would be asked to sit in on the tutorials, to become familiar with the work the child was doing and be able to help their child at home to consolidate their learning. The senior teacher prides herself on ensuring that children left the school after every session knowing that they had achieved or clarified an area of learning. She remarked that she liked to see the 'spring in the children's steps as they greeted their parents knowing they had a successful learning experience'.

The teaching observed in these complementary schools was good. The teachers were all knowledgeable and confident. The group teaching of English and maths at key stage 2 and 3 were particularly impressive. The teachers were enthusiastic and delivered the subject matter confidently. The children were engaged. They were given the opportunity to ask questions, contemplate possible answers and propose ideas. Teachers were knowledgeable about the children and their learning styles and could get children to use their existing knowledge to solve problems. The three teachers of English demonstrated their experience and knowledge, getting the children to use their skills to work through the tasks. One large language group was divided to work on two different exercises, a little cluster constructing a Haiku poem, the other working on a long comprehension piece about girls' football, while the teacher worked one to one with a child.

One teacher from Olive complementary school asserted that the circumstances prevented her from doing more differentiated work, yet the task the children were involved in was differentiated and a successful match to their skills. It was evident that this teacher was setting extremely high standards for herself as well as the children in her class.

Discipline and class management did not feature as a major issue in any of the schools we visited. Occasionally a teacher would call a child's name and ask them to lower their voice or to get back on task. One experienced male teacher provided a running commentary on the class, as in this example:

> Kamari, I am sure Taya does not need your eyes on his page just now, as he is trying to finish his math so that I can mark it before he goes home. I want to see how many problems you have left to do. As soon as I am finished with Marisa here, I'll be coming to see you. (Turning to another child absorbed in her work) By the way, Elisha, good going, you have worked out that really tough problem, keep going man ... good, good.

This teacher demonstrated particularly insightful rapport with his group. Before anybody needed 'reminding' to remain on task, he made it clear to the children that he knew what was going on – all the time.

It was evident from our observations that the teachers in all the schools we visited knew the children and their needs and learning styles and that they used the knowledge to motivate and extend the children's learning. The case study of Aubrey, presented below, illustrates how a complementary school can transform a child's education and hence life chances.

Aubrey's story

Aubrey came from the Caribbean in 2004 when he was 14. He had been a 'good' student at a 'good' school and was expected to attain 'good' O and A levels. He was ambitious, wanting to study sciences so he could become a doctor. Sharing her son's aspirations and wanting to ensure continuity for his academic studies, his mother researched schools in her area and decided against the local school. She succeeded in securing a place for him in a 'good' vibrant school in north London.

Aubrey arrived in school and applied himself to his studies. He was a quiet student, not used to speaking out in class. Back in the Caribbean, students waited for the teacher to point to a pupil and ask a direct factual question which required a clear 'right' answer. In London, Aubrey encountered a totally different style of classroom management and teaching style. Here he was expected to demonstrate his enthusiasm for learning, volunteer answers and actively participate in class discussions without necessarily waiting for the teacher to point to him. Equally he was expected to present his opinions in his written assignments and to raise questions and arguments. Aubrey found himself being belittled by the teacher and teased by other pupils. His self-esteem 'took a dive' his confidence began to waver, he became even more silent in class.

Aubrey's mother noticed the change in her son and got on the case. Her first action was to talk to a teacher she knew, who was the director of Progressive supplementary school. She signed Aubrey up initially for individual tutorials and then to attend the Saturday school.

The inside knowledge of the teachers at Progressive, their knowledge of the racialised expectations teachers hold of black children, and particularly of black boys, and the differences in class management and teaching styles enabled Progressive to quickly diagnose what was happening to Aubrey and what should be done about it.

His mother challenged the mainstream school's practices, knowing that she was treading a fine line between alienating the school towards her son and antagonising teachers – which could exacerbate their racialised behaviour – and work against putting matters right.

Aubrey and his mother decided not to tell the school about his attendance at Progressive. Progressive's 'survival plan' for Aubrey entailed boosting his self confidence, teaching him additional study skills, including verbal as well as written strategies. Progressive teachers as well as his mother armoured Aubrey with the information that some teachers held low expectations and were guilty of stereotypical thinking about black pupils. His mother's challenge of the school and her unwavering support of her son, especially her steadfastness regarding his academic ability, ensured that Aubrey was entered into the right GCSE examination band.

With the help of his mother's vigilance and the academic support of at the Progressive school, Aubrey survived his short stay in secondary education in England. He attained A stars in his science GCSEs and was on his way to study medicine at Imperial College in London. He even found time to return to Progressive as a volunteer teacher.

Chapter 6 describes the CILT research and the following two their findings about the aspirations of the teachers in the complementary schools they studied. The CILT findings complement those of our own project, presented in Chapter 9. Together these studies present a compelling picture of complementary schools in England today and a solid basis for the recommendations which conclude the book.

PART THREE
The CILT Project

6
The CILT schools and the research methodology

In the questionnaires we sent to schools we asked teachers about their qualifications and subject expertise as well as their training needs. The responses we had were positive overall. The teachers who had responded knew where to progress in their careers and their own training needs. Most of the teachers we interviewed said they wished to work in mainstream schools but were not sure how to go about it. Some mentioned the training offered by the National Resource Centre for supplementary schools and said that found it helpful. The research commissioned by CILT explores the issues in detail and is the subject of the next two chapters.

At the time Tözün and Claudette commenced their research, Tözün also joined the project team based at the Institute for Policy Studies in Education at London Metropolitan University, which CILT had commissioned to explore the qualifications of complementary school teachers and to identify the barriers they faced in obtaining QTS. We constantly evaluated the progression of the CILT project and and our own, sharing our findings and experiences. Both projects progressed harmoniously as both had an interest in the aspirations of complementary school teachers. So we discussed the issues and shared information freely. The methodology and findings of the projects were very similar. Consequently, rather than presenting the findings of the CILT project in different parts of this book, we are presenting its key findings in this section thus extending CILT's reach and helping readers to contextualise the findings of our own research that we are also presenting.

Our Languages: Teachers in Supplementary Schools and their Aspirations to Teach Community Languages was commissioned by CILT, The National Centre for Languages. The consortium manager was Sarah Cartwright, and the Project Team, based at IPSE, London Metropolitan University was Sarah Minty, Uvanney Maylor, Tözün Issa, Kuyok Kuyok and Alistair Ross.

The full report can be found at http://www.cilt.org.uk/commlangs/our_langs/londonmet_report.pdf

Aims of the CILT project

This research was designed to:

1. Determine how many teachers in supplementary schools would wish to obtain UK Qualified Teaching Status (QTS), and how many of these would seek to work as teachers in mainstream education, in what capacity, and which subject and phase they would aspire to teach; and what barriers they face (or perceive they face) to obtaining QTS.

2. Determine the training and other needs this group might have, whether preparatory to one of the existing QTS routes, or possibly through some alternative QTS route, in light of their current qualifications and experience.

3. Devise and deliver courses or other appropriate actions or materials that would address these needs.

In the initial phase of the project (to March 31 2008) a pilot study was conducted in seven neighbouring London LEAs to scope aims 1 and 2 above in the locality. The final study focused on seven local authorities in north London: Kensington and Chelsea, Westminster, Camden, Islington, Haringey, Hackney and Waltham Forest. They were chosen because they were contiguous and had a substantial proportion of nearly all Britain's main minority ethnic groups, enabling the team to access sufficient different communities for their purpose. This geographical area was chosen not as a representative sample but rather as an area that had the required range of ethnic representation and because it would be geographically suited to be a recruitment area for any putative course organised at London Metropolitan University.

Table 6.1 shows the percentage of pupils by ethnicity in primary and secondary maintained schools in five of these seven LAs, compared to all of Inner London and all England levels. These figures suggested that a study of supplementary schools in this area would produce a wide enough range of groups, and generally of sufficient size, to ensure that many types of community would be represented among the schools we found.

The sampling method

Contacts in each of the authorities chosen were approached, either directly through known contacts or through the LAs' websites, so the researchers could develop a database of all the supplementary schools in each authority. Not all the LAs could provide complete lists and the accuracy of some of the lists was questionable. The low return rates achieved reflected the inadequacy of the LA's knowledge and perhaps indicates the amount of interest the authorities take in their supplementary schools.

From the lists the LAs provided or the research team compiled, a database was ultimately developed. It contained a total of 213 institutions across the seven London boroughs.

Survey packs were sent to the headteacher of each supplementary school on the database. These contained a letter explaining the research, a questionnaire to be filled in by the headteacher and five copies of a teacher questionnaire (see Appendix 2). Headteachers were requested to complete and return the headteacher questionnaire, and to distribute the other questionnaires to their teaching staff. Headteachers were also asked to request additional forms should they need them. Each survey was provided with a pre-paid envelope in which to return to the questionnaires.

It was hoped that a snowballing technique could also be used in the distribution: those who were sent a questionnaire were invited to identify other supplementary school teachers they knew, and either pass a copy of the questionnaire on to them or give details so they could be

Table 6.1: Primary and Secondary Pupils by Ethnicity: England, Inner London, and the Kensington and Chelsea, Westminster, Camden, Islington and Hackney LEAs, January 2007

	Primary			Secondary			Numbers of pupils in 5LAs
	England	Inner London	5 LAs	England	Inner London	5LAs	
White British	77.0	21.6	22.6	80.4	22.7	25.9	19,580
Irish	0.4	1.0	1.4	0.4	1.2	1.9	1,340
Traveller of Irish Heritage	0.1	0.1	0.19	0.0	0.1	0.1	130
Gypsy/Roma	0.2	0.1	0.1	0.1	0.1	0.1	40
Any other White background	3.1	10.7	14.7	2.5	9.5	12.7	11,300
White & Black Caribbean	1.2	3.4	3.2	1.0	2.9	3.0	2,560
White & Black African	0.4	1.2	1.3	0.3	1.0	1.2	1,030
White & Asian	0.8	0.8	0.9	0.6	0.7	0.9	730
Any other mixed background	1.3	3.8	4.9	0.9	2.9	3.8	3,610
Indian	2.4	2.6	2.1	2.4	3.1	1.9	1,670
Pakistani	3.5	2.8	0.9	2.6	3.2	1.2	820
Bangladeshi	1.5	11.6	8.4	1.0	11.3	7.5	6,550
Any other Asian background	1.1	2.0	1.4	0.9	2.3	1.9	1,320
Black Caribbean	1.4	10.3	8.5	1.3	10.5	7.9	6,760
Black African	2.7	17.1	15.6	2.0	16.7	16.1	12,910
Any other Black background	0.5	3.1	2.4	0.4	2.9	2.2	1,740
Chinese	0.3	0.7	0.7	0.4	1.0	1.0	690
Any other ethnic group	1.2	6.1	10.4	1.0	6.2	9.2	8,100

Source: DCSF: Schools and Pupils in England: January 2007: Tables 32 and 33: Maintained primary and secondary schools: number and percentage of pupils by ethnic group

sent a questionnaire in the hope of reaching more people. But no school requested further questionnaires or headteachers' packs.

A trial questionnaire was piloted in December 2007 with a small number of headteachers and teachers in three of the seven local authorities. In light of the pilot, minor amendments were made to the questionnaire. Headteachers' packs were sent to schools at the beginning of January 2008, with requests for the surveys to be returned to the research team by the end of the month. A reminder was sent to all schools that had not responded by the end of January.

The response rate

The main phase of the research was conducted between January and February 2008. In most teacher surveys, we would anticipate that if 1000 forms are distributed to teachers, we would get about 400 responses. However, in this case the forms were not distributed directly to teachers, as there were no means of gaining access to them, but through the headteachers who became gatekeepers. Probably not all headteachers would distribute the forms to their staff and not all schools would have as many as five teachers. So it is not possible to calculate how many of the teacher questionnaires reached teachers.

The number of responses to both the teacher and headteacher surveys was nonetheless disappointing. Of the 213 headteachers' packs sent out to schools, only 20 were returned. It became evident that some of the addresses where packs were sent to were not supplementary schools at all – about six contacted the project team to report this. This figure may conceal many more institutions that are not schools. A further 16 packs were returned by the post office. So an apparent response rate of just 10 per cent may be an underestimate of the true rate of return. A total of 54 responses were received from teachers, but it is not possible to suggest what response rate this represents: just that it is certainly more than 5 per cent.

The responses received from headteachers and teachers represented 30 schools in all, six of the seven local authorities. The teachers represented 21 schools and the headteachers 20. Nine schools had responses from both teachers and headteachers. No responses were received from Westminster – but only four schools there had been identified in the database.

Table 6.2

	Packs distributed	Responses from Headteachers	Responses from Teachers	Focus Group Partici-pants
Camden	30	1	7	6
Hackney	29	4	10	5
Haringey	28	2	1	-
Islington	60	5	12	-
Kensington & Chelsea	29	1	5	-
Waltham Forest	33	6	17	5
Westminster	4	-	-	-
Missing data	-	-	2	-
Total	213	19	54	16

Issues relating to the low response rate

In the original proposal for this research some of the potential difficulties in conducting research with supplementary school teachers were considered. The supplementary schools do not necessarily fall neatly within the confines of a single LA, so the sample area inevitably has some imprecision. There is no accurate or central register of all supplementary schools, let alone of the teachers in them. So the project team had to rely on lists provided by local authorities and other contacts working in the supplementary schools. Whilst lists of schools were obtained for each local authority it was debatable just, how complete, accurate and up to date these were. The LAs from whom more responses were received tended to be the authorities whose lists were most complete.

The only way of gaining access to teachers depended on the headteachers passing on the questionnaires to their staff. As we found in our own study, it is likely that a significant number did not pass on the questionnaires and ask the teachers to complete them. There are several possible reasons for this:

■ generally, the headteachers are themselves overwhelmed with tasks and demands

- many heads may wish to protect their staff from additional burdens
- some headteachers may not have wanted their staff to participate in the research, either because they had misgivings about more of their staff perhaps obtaining QTS; or
- for fear of losing their staff to mainstream schools
- some heads see their schools as outside mainstream education, so assumed that the survey was not relevant to them.

The project team telephoned the non-responding headteachers with whom some previous contact had been made to explore their reasons for not responding. It was found that, in addition to the responses listed above, some headteachers had confused this questionnaire with the rather similar survey of supplementary schools that we carried out earlier.

The team identified a number of reasons why teachers did not return the questionnaire: those who already had QTS may have considered it irrelevant, and felt no need to respond (although one third of the teachers responding did already have QTS); some would not have had the time or inclination (as with other surveys, to which 60 per cent of teachers generally do not respond); some may have had objections to the survey and its intentions; some teachers will have been suspicious about supplying information of a personal nature.

The questionnaires

CILT distributed two separate questionnaires: a Headteacher Survey and a Teacher Survey.

The Headteachers' questionnaires consisted of a short two sides of A4, designed to elicit contextual data about supplementary schools; about both the school and the teachers. It asked about the size of the school, details about the children and communities it taught, and the languages and curriculum taught at the school. The headteachers were asked also about the number of teachers in the school, the number with QTS, and questions relating to the recruitment and retention of teachers in their schools.

The Teachers' questionnaire was slightly longer, covering four sides of a folded A3 sheet. It sought information on the following:

- where the person teaches, what they teach, who they teach, and the extent of their teaching workload

- their educational background: qualifications, when and where obtained, if QTS is already held; any attempts to gain QTS

- desire (or not) to obtain UK QTS and their reasons

- intention or desire to work in maintained schools if QTS obtained? If so, what kind of work would they expect to undertake in a maintained school?

- self-identification of further study or qualifications required; whether they have taken steps towards acquiring these

- demographic background: their age, gender, ethnicity, languages spoken and proficiency in said languages, birthplace and nationality.

In addition, the respondents were asked:

- whether they would be interested in being sent details in future of possible courses that might help lead towards QTS, and

- whether they would be willing to participate in a focus group to discuss issues raised in the questionnaire.

The questionnaires consisted of closed questions, multiple choices (tick box, Likert scales, etc) and open-ended questions that required coding.

Focus Groups

To complement and explore in more detail the data from the two questionnaires, focus groups were set up. The participants were self-selecting, having indicated in the Teachers' Survey that they would like to be involved and providing contact details.

Although there were relatively few responses to the Teachers' Survey, those who did respond showed great interest in participating in the focus groups. More than two-thirds (34 teachers) were prepared to be involved in a group. All of them were approached by the project team and offered a range of dates, and three focus groups were set up. It was anticipated that only one focus group would be held, but the high number of people willing to be involved, coupled with the low level of quantitative data made it attractive to organise three groups.

The focus groups met at London Metropolitan University in the early evening, with 16 participants in each (five headteachers and 11 teachers of whom five were derived from one school). An additional individual teacher interview was conducted face-to-face. These were all teaching in supplementary schools in Camden, Islington and Waltham Forest.

The discussion schedule designed for the focus groups covered similar themes to those in the Teachers' Survey and was extended to explore these themes in more detail. Participants were asked about the English educational system (such as what they particularly like or dislike about it) and about the difficulties they encountered in seeking QTS.

Analysis

The questionnaire data was coded and checked. Frequency counts and cross-tabs were run for both the Teacher Survey and the Headteacher Survey. The focus group discussions and the interview were transcribed and coded prior to being analysed in detail.

Findings from the research

Both the quantitative and qualitative findings from the research follow. They are set out in four sections:

- the schools and the communities they serve, and headteachers' views of the staffing in their schools
- the teachers, their educational background, qualifications, experience and aspirations relating to QTS
- the teachers' languages and abilities and whether they wished to teach languages should they obtain QTS
- issues relating to obtaining QTS, the perceived barriers to doing so, and any additional skills that teachers perceive as necessary for them to acquire before obtaining QTS.

The schools and their communities

The key features of the supplementary schools in the sample are outlined below: the characteristics of the school, the communities it serves and the curriculum covered. Staffing issues, including the length of time teachers stay at the schools and headteachers' opinions on the recruitment and retention of their staff are also considered.

Survey respondents were given the option of writing the name of their supplementary school at the top of the questionnaire. Most teachers and headteachers did so; only one headteacher and four teachers left this blank.

Thirty schools were represented by these teachers and headteachers. Eight teachers from one school responded to the Teacher Survey, but such a high number was unusual. Four responses were received from teachers in each of two schools; three teachers each from six schools; two teachers each from three schools; and just a single teacher from eight of the schools.

The responses from the teachers or headteachers from six of the seven local authorities were sampled. The greatest number of responses came from both headteachers and teachers in Waltham Forest (six head-teachers and 17 teachers), followed by Islington (six headteachers and 12 teachers). The lists of schools provided by both these authorities appeared to be unusually complete, and their accuracy may have helped to ensure a better response rate, notwithstanding the absence of West-minster.

Table 6.3

Location of school	No. teachers	% teachers	No. headteachers	% headteachers
Islington	12	22	6	30
Kensington & Chelsea	5	9	1	5
Camden	7	13	1	5
Hackney	10	18	4	20
Haringey	1	2	2	10
Waltham Forest	17	31	6	30
Westminster	-	-	-	-
Missing	2	4	-	-
N	54		20	

The focus groups consisted primarily of teachers and a few head-teachers who represented a range of supplementary schools in three of the seven boroughs (Camden, Islington and Waltham Forest).

In the survey, headteachers reported that their schools ranged in terms of size from less than 25 pupils (four schools) to those with more than 100 (five schools). The highest proportion of headteachers (eight schools) reported that their school had 50-100 pupils

Table 6.4

School Size	schools	%
Less than 25 pupils	4	20
25-50 pupils	3	15
50-100 pupils	8	40
More than 100 pupils	5	25
N	20	

Both questionnaires asked about the age groups taught in the supplementary schools. All the schools represented by the headteachers taught primary children aged 5-11, and a large majority also taught 11-16 year olds (18 schools). Fewer headteachers reported that their school taught 16-18 year olds (seven schools), and adults or under 5s (four and three schools respectively). Similarly, the majority of teachers reported

Table 6.5

Age groups taught by teachers/in the school	No. teachers	% teachers	No. headteachers	% headteachers
Under 5s	4	7	3	15
5-11 year olds	44	81	20	100
11-16 year olds	32	59	18	90
16-18 year olds	14	26	7	35
Adults	3	6	4	20
N	54		20	

that they taught 5-11 year olds (44 teachers), while more than half reported that they taught 11-16 year olds (32 teachers). Fewer teachers taught 16-18 year olds, adults and the under 5s. All teachers responded that they taught their pupils in mixed age classes.

Echoing the findings of the questionnaire data, the focus group participants all reported that they taught both primary and secondary school aged children. All focus group participants were currently teaching in supplementary schools catering for both primary and secondary aged pupils, but some had specific responsibilities for pupils aged, for example, 5 to 6 or 8 to10. These schools had between five and seven teachers, catering for between 60 and 100 pupils, with individual teachers managing classes of 18 to 20 pupils.

Headteachers were asked to specify how classes were organised in the school. Most reported that their schools taught pupils through a combination of styles and approaches; more than two thirds of headteachers chose more than one option (14 headteachers). The majority of schools grouped children by age (14 schools), while twelve schools grouped (or also grouped) pupils by ability. Half the headteachers reported that children in their schools were grouped according to their language competence.

Table 6.6

How classes are organised		
	No of schools	% schools
Taught by age	14	70
Taught by ability	12	60
Taught by language competence	10	50
Other	2	10
N	20	

School communities

The majority of headteachers (14) reported that their school served a particular community. The communities identified by headteachers included (in alphabetical order):

■ African-Caribbean and other black pupils

- Bangladeshi
- Cabindan [Angolan]
- Chinese
- Ethiopian
- Eritrean
- Greek
- Hungarian
- Polish
- Somali
- Turkish and/or Kurdish
- Schools which served general multicultural and inclusive communities, or no particular communities

The communities identified by the headteachers were subsequently coded into seven groups: African; African-Caribbean, Asian, European, Turkish, and those which stated that they served no particular community but were multicultural. The largest proportion of headteachers responding to the survey came from African schools (six headteachers), followed by those who identified their schools as serving multicultural areas, or no specific community (three for each group). Headteachers representing schools serving the Asian (two), European (three) and Turkish (two) communities also responded to the survey, as did one headteacher from a school serving the African-Caribbean community.

Table 6.7

Type of community served by school		
	Number of schools	% schools
African	6	30
African-Caribbean	1	5
Asian	2	10
European	3	15
Turkish	2	10
Multi-cultural	3	15
No community	3	15
N	20	

Focus group participants represented schools serving similarly varied communities, such as Latin American (eg Columbian/Venezuelan), Ethiopian, Eritrean, Somali, Ghanaian, Sudanese, Pakistani and Hungarian communities.

Headteachers were also asked about the geographical locations their supplementary schools served. These were fairly wide ranging, with some restricted to the borough in the which the school was situated, and others serving surrounding boroughs or larger areas of London. One headteacher indicated that his school served 'London and the Home Counties'.

Curriculum covered by the CILT schools

Both headteachers and teachers were asked to select from a list which aspects were covered by their school. Similar proportions of headteachers and teachers indicated that their schools broadly taught NC subjects, mother tongue and culture and heritage. Approximately three-quarters of both teachers and headteachers (80% and 70% respectively) indicated that their school taught the national curriculum.

Mother tongue classes were also covered in more than half the supplementary schools: 59 per cent of the teachers', and 65 per cent of the headteachers' schools. Culture and heritage was covered in approximately two-fifths of the schools (52% teachers and 45% headteachers). Fewer headteachers and teachers reported that Religious studies was covered in their supplementary schools (15% teachers and 25% headteachers). Other aspects which were covered by the schools included

Table 6.8

What areas does the school cover?				
	No. teachers	% teachers	No. headteachers	% headteachers
National Curriculum	43	80	14	70
Mother Tongue	32	59	13	65
Culture and Heritage	28	52	9	45
Religious Studies	8	15	5	25
Other	14	26	7	35
N	54		20	

sport, working with parents, emotional literacy, and activities relating to culture such as traditional singing and dancing.

Schools generally covered more than one of these categories. Over half the teachers (34 or 63%) said their school covered more than one category, with 15 teachers reporting that their school covered four or five. Similarly, three-quarters of headteachers reported that their schools covered more than one of these areas, with four schools covering four.

Most numerous were the schools which addressed national curriculum subjects. The headteachers were asked to state which subjects were covered in their schools and all who did so named maths and English, while two-thirds taught science and a third taught languages.

What areas of the National Curriculum are covered?

Table 6.9

Areas of the National Curriculum taught in your school		
	No. headteachers	% headteachers
Mathematics	15	100
English	15	100
Sciences	10	67
Languages	5	33
Other	4	27
N	15	

Teachers were also asked to write in an open question what subjects they taught at their school. Their entries were then coded and analysed. More than half the teachers reported that they taught languages and maths, a third taught English.

Generally, the teachers reported teaching a mixture of subjects in their schools. Almost two-thirds of (33) said they taught more than one subject and seven teachers taught four or five. A quarter indicated that the only subject they currently teach is languages or mother tongue. 'Other' subjects taught by the teachers included sport, martial arts, dancing, singing, running workshops for parents, and providing advice on confidential matters.

Table 6.10

What subject do you teach in your supplementary school?

	No. of teachers	% teachers
Mathematics	29	54
Sciences	15	28
English	18	33
Languages	30	56
Humanities/ Social Studies	1	2
Religious Studies	4	7
ICT	1	2
Culture and heritage	6	11
Other	9	17
N	54	

This kind of mixing by the schools of the types of subjects was confirmed in the focus group discussions. All the participants taught a combination of core national curriculum subjects (English, mathematics, sciences), mother tongue classes (eg Amharic, Tigrigna, Moru, Hungarian, Somali, Akan and Ga) and cultural/heritage/identity (eg home country history, dance, music) in their schools. A group of Latin American teachers taught Spanish and Latin American culture. None of the focus group participants specifically mentioned teaching religious studies.

Staffing issues

The length of time which teachers had worked in their current supplementary school varied, although most headteachers reported that their staff taught in their school for at least three years (11 headteachers).

The teachers were asked how long they had worked in their supplementary schools. Their replies ranged from three months to 26 years (mean 7 years, median 4 years). Most focus group participants had worked in their supplementary schools for at least a year. One teacher had worked at his school for nine years until 2006, when the funding for the school 'ran out'. There were several examples of teachers with three or more years' experience. Two supplementary school headteachers had been running their supplementary schools for seven years or more.

Table 6.11

Length of time teachers stay at the school		
	No. headteachers	% headteachers
Less than one year	2	10
1-2 years	4	20
3-5 years	8	40
5 years or more	5	25
Missing	1	5
N	20	

The Headteacher survey asked respondents how many teachers worked in their school. The number working in the schools ranged from only one teacher to 39 (a mean of nine teachers, median six).

Heads were asked how many of their teachers had qualified teacher status. In some schools there were none, while in one school all eight teachers had QTS, and in another 33 (a mean of 4.5 teachers and median of three).

From these two questions, the proportion of teachers with QTS in schools can be calculated. The range was from 0 to 100 per cent (mean 53%, median 41%).

Recruitment and retention of teachers

Headteachers were asked specific questions about the recruitment and retention of teachers in their schools in order to better understand staffing issues in supplementary schools. Respondents were asked to indicate whether they agreed, disagreed (or neither) with a range of statements.

The headteachers were divided as to whether they agreed with the statement 'I do not have a problem recruiting teachers'. Respondents were more in agreement about some of the factors which make recruitment difficult. Resources and funding appeared to be the key issues, with the majority of headteachers agreeing with the statements 'I don't have sufficient resources to take on more classes' (16) and 'I can only afford to employ a small number of staff' (14). Three quarters of headteachers disagreed that the location of the school made it difficult to attract staff (13), but there was less agreement over the impact that the times the school operated had on recruiting teachers (nine head-teachers agreed).

Three of the statements related to training and qualifications. Whilst equal numbers of teachers agreed and disagreed with the statement 'Those who apply do not have sufficient training / experience', more than half agreed that 'There is a shortage of teachers with qualifications' and 'There is a shortage of language specialists'.

Table 6.12

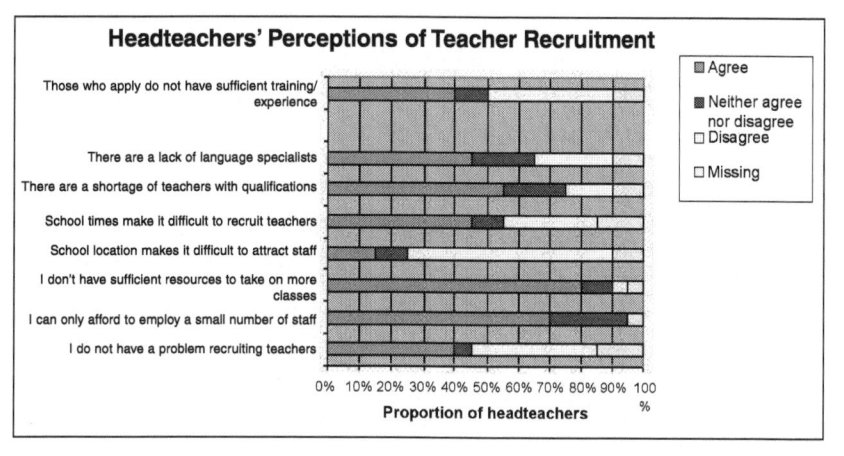

Heads were asked for their perceptions about the retention of teachers in their schools. More than half (11) agreed with the statement that they had no problem retaining teachers. The key problem in retention was funding, with 14 headteachers agreeing that 'Insufficient funding makes it difficult to retain teachers'. Headteachers largely disagreed that they lost teachers to mainstream schools (12 disagreed), that 'Teachers leave to concentrate on other commitments' (10), and that 'A heavy workload discourages teachers from staying' (8). Responses were mixed in relation to the statements that 'Teachers leave for other work / to develop other skills' and that 'Teachers leave because they don't have up-to-date resources'.

Teachers' qualifications and experience

The teachers were considered in relation to the supplementary schools in which they work – the hours they worked, the subjects they taught. But first the broad characteristics of the teachers who responded to the teacher survey were looked at: their ethnicity, country of origin and nationality were analysed and so were their educational background and qualifications and their teaching experience in the UK and abroad. These are described in the next chapter.

7

The teachers in the CILT schools

The CILT Project team collected information from the teachers' survey about their personal characteristics. There were more women than men in the sample (24 men to 28 women) but this is still a significantly larger proportion of men than the proportion teaching children of this age in the mainstream. The teachers ranged widely in age but most were aged 30-44, which matches the profile of the mainstream teaching force.

Teachers were asked (in an optional open question) to describe their ethnic background, as this was felt to be a more appropriate way of asking for the information than the standardised extended categories used in the census and elsewhere. It was hoped that in this way we would capture the diversity of ethnicities of people working in supplementary schools. The majority of respondents (39 teachers) answered the question. A breakdown of their responses is provided in Table 7.1.

Teachers were asked which country they were born in and their nationality. Twenty-seven different countries were represented in the returns, including eight sub-Saharan African countries, one in North Africa, four South American countries, two in the Caribbean, four Asian countries, three in eastern Europe, four in western Europe plus the UK. Eighteen different nationalities were identified by the teachers; just under half (21) were British citizens.

Table 7.1: The Teachers' Nationalities

(census category)	(sub-category)	(country)	n	%
	African		4	7.5
	Black African		4	7.5
	African (Nigerian)		1	2
		Eritrean	1	2
		Somali (Black)	1	2
Afro-Caribbean			1	2
Black Caribbean			1	2
		Morrocan	1	2
	North African (Moroccan)		1	2
		Arab	1	2
	British African		1	2
	British Indian		1	2
		Latin American	1	2
		Latino American	1	2
Asian			2	4
		Pakistani	2	4
		Asian Pakistani	1	2
		Bangladeshi	6	11
		Bengali	1	2
		Asian Bengali	1	2
		Asian-Bangladsehi	1	2
		Turkish	3	6
		Turkish Cypriots	2	4
White			2	4
		White Hungarian	1	2
		Hungarian	1	2
		Greek White	1	2
	White European		1	2

Teachers and their supplementary schools

Almost all the teachers reported that they taught at their supplementary schools on Saturdays (93%). A much smaller proportion teach at their schools on Sundays and/or after school. The focus group participants operated mostly only on Saturdays, with one also offering evening sessions two evenings a week.

Table 7.2

When do you teach at supplementary school?		
	No. teachers	% teachers
Teach after school	7	13
Teach Saturdays	50	93
Teach Sundays	8	15
N	54	

The teacher survey also asked how many hours per week the teachers taught at their supplementary schools. This ranged from two hours (12) to 12 hours (1 teacher) per week (mean 4 hours per week; median 3 hours).

Qualifications and experience

Teachers were asked to indicate the levels of their qualifications and where and when they qualified. Twenty five (46%) had a degree as their highest level of qualification, while nineteen (35%) had a post-graduate qualification. A further 32 teachers (59%) indicated that they had a teaching qualification as well. Only four teachers (7%) said GCSE and A levels was their highest qualification or their equivalents.

Most teachers with a degree said they had gained it outside Europe (27 out of the 38 teachers who identified the country where they received their degree). In contrast, of the nineteen teachers who had a post-graduate qualification, twelve had obtained it in the UK. The country where teaching qualifications were obtained varied from the UK (13), to Europe (4) and elsewhere (10), as was the case for the GCSEs or their equivalents. Most of the teachers who provided details of their qualifications had obtained them over ten years ago.

The focus group participants were a mix of qualified teachers (eg teaching qualification gained in country of origin – Columbia, Venezuela, Ghana, Ethiopia, Eritrea and one a teaching certificate from the UK) and people who had worked as unqualified teachers before coming to the UK. One, for example, had a 'high school qualification in teaching'.

In addition to teaching qualifications, some teachers had gained degrees in art, modern languages, business, humanities and other qualifications overseas. One had an engineering degree from the UK, and two had studied other courses in Britain such as ICT and English. The others had completed a course in community language teaching in north London. One is currently undertaking a counselling course. Some respondents had obtained various postgraduate qualifications in the UK.

Teaching experience outside the UK

A large proportion of teachers responding to the teacher survey indicated that they had experience of teaching outside the UK (37). This varied greatly, ranging from 3 months to 30 years. The mean number of years spent teaching was 7.25 years and the median was 5. Their teaching experience was acquired in 25 different countries. Most of those who had experience of teaching abroad had worked in primary and secondary schools but some had worked in further and higher education or in the private sector.

Table 7.3

Where did you teach?		
	No. of teachers	% teachers
Primary school	17	43
Secondary school	18	46
College	6	15
University	1	3
Other	14	36
N	39	

Most of the teachers indicated that they had been teachers in their home country (25 out of 37). Six had previously been headteachers. Some wrote that they had worked as private tutors abroad.

Teachers who indicated they had teaching experience outside the UK were asked what subjects they had taught. Almost half had taught languages (24), while a third had taught mathematics. The languages included Arabic, Bengali, Ga (a Ghanaian language), Urdu, English, Hungarian, Polish, and Spanish languages.

Table 7.4

What subject(s) did you teach?		
	No. of teachers	% teachers
Mathematics	18	47
Sciences	14	37
Languages	24	63
Humanities/Social Studies	10	26
Religious Studies	11	29
ICT	4	10
Other	3	8
N	38	

Most of the focus group members had worked in primary/elementary schools before coming to the UK. The length of overseas teaching experience ranged from one to seventeen years.

Two teachers of African heritage had one and seventeen years teaching experience in Ethiopia and Ghana respectively and both had taught in secondary schools but only one had a teaching degree. A Hungarian heritage teacher had taught Hungarian as a foreign language in Hungary for six years.

Amongst the Latin American group of teachers, one was a qualified geography and history teacher and had taught for two years in a secondary school in Columbia, whilst a primary teacher had taught art and Spanish, and a third had taught modern language in primary school. Only one of the Latin American teachers had no teaching qualification or experience of teaching in her country of origin. Apart from their teaching qualifications and experience from abroad, a few teachers had also worked voluntarily or in a paid capacity as classroom or teaching assistants in mainstream UK schools. For example:

> I'm a graduate from India. I've been living in this country for 19 years and I've worked in several schools as a classroom assistant ... I really enjoyed working with the children (inaudible). I've got a huge experience of working in the classroom one to one with a teacher. (Indian woman)

> I am teaching Urdu on a voluntary basis (Pakistani woman)

One respondent had started by working as a voluntary teaching assistant, then took a teaching assistant course. She said this helped her gain employment in her daughter's school, where she has been working as a teaching assistant for nearly four years. Another respondent had previously worked as a science technician for seven years before embarking on a PGCE course. Working as teaching assistants or technicians had provided this group with insights into the British education system. One respondent was already enrolled on a PGCE science course.

Language and capacity

This section analyses the languages taught in the schools, the teachers' language qualifications, and their proficiency in the various languages.

Languages taught in the supplementary schools:
The Headteachers' Survey

The Headteachers' Survey asked respondents to list the languages taught in their schools. There was a fairly even spread between headteachers who reported that their schools taught community languages (7 schools); English (5 schools); and those who taught a mix of community, modern foreign languages and English (7 schools).

Of the 20 schools represented in the Headteacher Survey, twelve offered English, either alone or in combination with another language. A further thirteen languages were identified as being taught in the supplementary schools. Although most headteachers indicated that only one language was taught in their school, a few offered more than one – four schools taught two languages and one taught four (English, French, Spanish and German).

The languages the teachers spoke and their qualifications

Just over half the respondents to the Teachers' Survey indicated that they were qualified to teach a language (28 out of 54). Of these, 26 provided further details of the languages they were qualified to teach, identifying 18 different languages. These can be grouped into modern foreign languages; community languages; English; those who were qualified to teach a mix of MFL, community languages, and/or English; and those who indicated they were qualified to teach other languages such as Latin and ancient Greek.

The majority of those qualified to teach languages were qualified to teach community languages (17 teachers, 31%). Five teachers reported that they were qualified to teach a mix of languages (9%), while three said they could teach English (6%) and two were qualified to teach modern foreign languages (4%). Teachers were not required to identify their language qualifications but some indicated that they were qualified to teach a specific community language because of their fluency in what was their first language.

When asked about their level of language proficiency in English and other languages, almost all the teachers claimed to be at least 'fairly fluent' at speaking English and to have a 'fair understanding' of reading English, and a 'fair ability' in writing English. Two thirds of teachers reported that they were 'very strong' at reading English, while half spoke it 'very fluently' and almost two fifths had 'advanced ability' in writing English.

Three-quarters of the teachers spoke more than one language in addition to English. The average number was two languages, although four respondents indicated that they spoke five languages including English – mainly a combination of community and modern foreign languages.

Twenty-two different languages were spoken by the teachers of which the great majority were community languages – see table 7.5. Many of the CS teachers who did not have qualified teacher status in the UK were keen to obtain it. Their aspirations and the obstacles to fulfilling them are the subject of Chapter 8.

Table 7.5

Community Language	Modern foreign language	Other	No. of speakers
		Ancient Greek	1
Amharic			3
Arabic			4
Bengali			8
	French		6
	German		4
Greek			2
Gujerati			1
Hindi			3
Hungarian			3
	Italian		2
		Latin	1
Polish			1
Portuguese			1
Punjabi			1
Russian			1
Serbo-Croat			1
Somali			3
	Spanish		8
Tigrigna			2
Turkish			5
Urdu			7

8

The qualifications and aspirations of
the teachers in the CILT schools

This chapter summaries the findings of the CILT project team and the teachers' and headteachers' perceptions about obtaining QTS: whether they had tried to gain it, their reasons for seeking to do so, the barriers they perceive to obtaining it, and any skills or processes which they perceive as necessary to acquire beforehand.

Holding qualified teacher status

The Teacher Survey asked whether respondents had obtained UK qualified teacher status. Just under a third of the 52 teachers who responded to the question (16) indicated they already had QTS. Most had qualified in the past five years.

Of the 36 respondents who did not have QTS, twelve had tried to obtain it but failed. This was also true of one focus group participant. She explained that she had attempted to gain a place on a PGCE course but had been unsuccessful. The institution she applied to initially so delayed their response that by the time she was invited to interview all the places had been filled. This happened again at other institutions she subsequently tried. Another respondent had tried to undertake a Registered Teacher Programme, could not find a school that would take him, despite having his overseas qualifications verified by NARIC (the national agency responsible for information and advice on professional skills and qualifications) as suitable for work in a school when he had a CRB (Criminal Records Bureau) check to make sure that he had no previous convictions.

Aspiring to QTS

The Teacher Survey asked respondents whether they would like to obtain QTS and most who did not already have it indicated that they would (32 of 37). The project team believed that they were likely to get responses to the questionnaire from teachers who were keen to obtain QTS, and that it is unlikely that such a high proportion of all supplementary school teachers are interested in doing so. Five teachers indicated that they would not like to gain QTS, saying 'I do not have the time', or citing as reasons: 'full time work', 'not available' and 'because attending university'.

Only one of the focus group participants already had a teaching certificate from the UK. Most of the others wished to pursue a primary or secondary QTS course.

The respondents to the Teacher Survey who were interested in QTS were asked to agree, disagree (or neither) with a series of statements about why they wished to obtain the qualification. Nearly all the teachers who answered the question agreed that obtaining the QTS 'would help me teach my subject area better', and 'would enhance my job prospects' (28 teachers for both statements). Most teachers also agreed that 'It (QTS) provides an opportunity to gain a UK qualification' (27), and that 'I would like to teach in mainstream schools' (24), although slightly fewer agreed with these statements.

Table 8.1: Reasons for obtaining UK QT

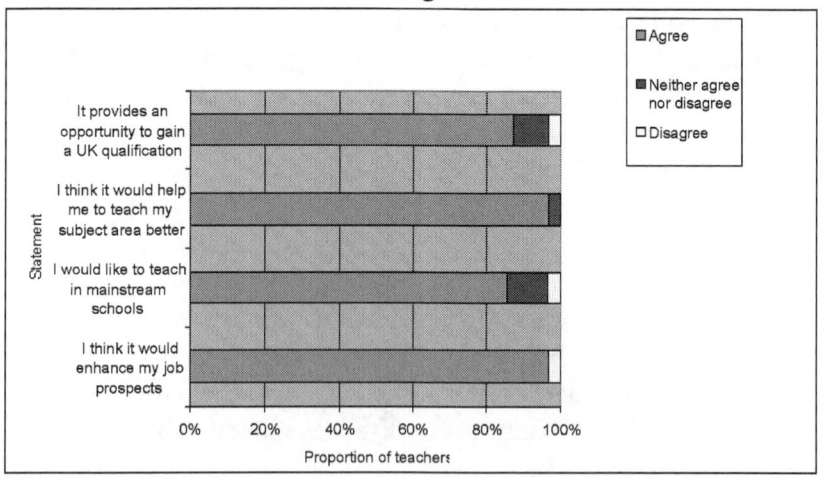

In the focus groups, participants also discussed their reasons for pursuing QTS. Teachers who attended said that they wished to obtain QTS so they could fulfil their ambition to become a teacher in England. They intended to use their qualification, once gained, to 'learn more [teaching] skills' and teach in mainstream schools. For example:

> I haven't had experience in teaching but I really enjoy it and really like to get a qualification of how to teach in primary school. (Columbian woman)

> I would like to work in the mainstream ... I used to teach back home primary kids. I have got several other qualifications and I am really interested to do this to learn more skills. (Indian woman)

Headteachers' perceptions of QTS

Headteachers were also asked about their teachers' aspiration to gain QTS. They generally agreed that that their staff would like to do so: thirteen thought that they would, and four were unsure.

Heads were also asked whether they agreed with two statements. Most headteachers agreed that: 'It would be good for my school if more teachers had QTS' (16). None disagreed but three did not answer the question. Fewer headteachers agreed with the statement that: 'My teachers would leave as soon as they acquire QTS'. Just under half of them disagreed (9) and only two agreed, while five neither agreed nor disagreed. Again, three respondents did not answer the question.

Table 8.2: Headteachers' Perceptions of QTS in their schools

Five headteachers attended the focus groups so they could represent the views of the teachers in their schools rather than their own. They were not interested in applying for QTS themselves but were keen to find out about different routes into teaching and other information they could pass on to their teachers who could not attend the sessions. There was a feeling amongst these headteachers that it would be a good thing for their staff to gain QTS, although some did express misgivings that they might then lose their teachers to the mainstream.

The teachers' intentions

The teachers were asked in what sector they would like to teach if they obtained their UK teaching qualification. Secondary and primary schools were most popular, with 14 and 12 teachers respectively choosing these options. Working in early years settings and further education were less popular.

Table 8.3

Where do you want to teach?		
	No. of teachers	% teachers
Early years settings	6	19
Primary school	12	37
Secondary school	17	53
Further education	13	40
Other	5	16
N	32	

The Teacher Survey asked what subjects the respondents would like to teach, were they to obtain QTS. More than two thirds indicated they would like to teach more than one subject (22 teachers), with most (14) choosing a combination of two subjects. The most popular subjects selected by teachers that they wished to teach were languages and maths (21 and 20 respectively).

Table 8.4

What subject(s) would you like to teach when you have UK QTS?		
	No. of teachers	% teachers
Maths	20	61
Sciences	8	24
Languages	21	64
Humanities/ Social Sciences	6	18
Religious Studies	8	24
ICT	1	3
Other	3	9
N	33	

Only four teachers indicated that they would like to teach a language by itself; the great majority said that they would like to teach languages alongside another subject (17). The most popular subject with which to teach a language was maths (5), followed by humanities and social science subjects (4). Six teachers indicated they would like to teach languages with more than one other subject, generally a combination of maths, science and humanities or social science with a language. Two teachers wished to teach a language alongside religious studies. Four teachers were interested only in teaching maths, were they to obtain QTS.

Thirteen teachers talked about the languages they would like to teach, were they to obtain QTS. Both modern foreign and community languages were mentioned as well as English: Arabic, Spanish, Amharic, ancient Greek, English, Urdu, Hindi, Punjabi, Hungarian, Bengali and French. Four indicated they would like to teach English.

The focus group participants were also keen to teach languages. Those who said they wished to teach a community language in mainstream schools named the following: Spanish (as spoken in Columbia and Venezuela), Hungarian, Urdu, Somali, Amharic, Tigrinya (Eritrean), Moru (a Sudanese language), Akan and Ga (Ghanaian languages). Two teachers suggested combining teaching a community language with another subject (eg Spanish with geography and history; or Akan/Ga with citizenship), and one wanted to become a mathematics/physics teacher. One expressed a preference for teaching ICT, English and science, and said that if she taught a language this would be secondary. But, there was some scepticism over whether it would be possible to do a course which would allow them to learn to teach their respective languages in mainstream schools, particularly when the language in question, such as Akan or Hungarian, would be new to schools. As one Somali man remarked: 'I don't think they can manage to find a mainstream school for us to teach Somali'.

It's the same with Hungarian, how would this fit into mainstream? (Hungarian woman)

Three respondents were particularly concerned that preference was being given to financially supporting the funding of QTS community language courses to meet the needs of the Asian (Urdu) and Middle Eastern communities – ie Arabic language support – which they felt would diminish the number of places that would be available to gain QTS in other community languages.

Challenges to acquiring QTS

The teacher survey also looked at the issues relating to perceived barriers and the additional skills that would be required before enrolling on a QTS course. Those who were interested in obtaining QTS were asked to identify any barriers they perceived to their enrolling on a QTS course, and any additional skills they thought they might need to obtain before starting it. Teachers were presented with a set of statements relating to the issues involved and asked to indicate their level of agreement. They generally indicated disagreement with the statements about the perceived barriers to enrolling on QTS courses.

But the greatest issue appeared to be funding, with twelve out of 28 teachers agreeing with the statement 'I don't think funding is available'. There was less agreement with the statement 'I don't think my prior qualifications and experience will be recognised'; sixteen teachers out of 27 disagreed with this. The level of agreement to the statements 'I have other work commitments' and 'The courses are not flexible enough' were fairly spread, suggesting that although these did matter they were far less important than funding. Most respondents did not consider family responsibilities or immigration status to be an issue and these factors may not have been applicable to all the respondents.

Table 8.5: Perceived Barriers to Enrolling on UK QTS Course

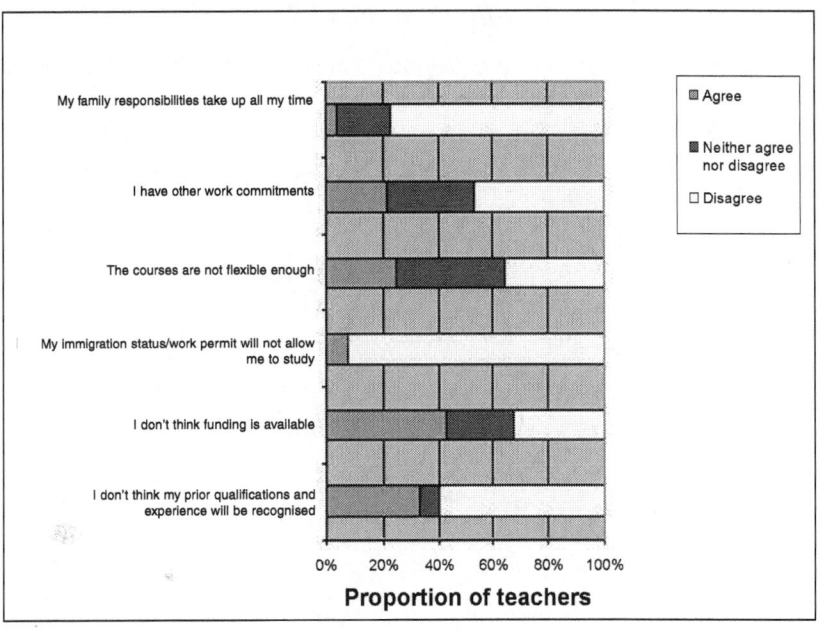

The barriers to qualifying were also discussed in the focus groups. Funding was considered to be a significant issue and the cost of undertaking a QTS course was mentioned. They asked questions such as 'How much is it going to be? Is it going to be expensive?' and questioned their ability to pay for a course without some form of financial support:

> I think the problem for me is the money that I need to do the course of turning teacher because I need to work to pay the rent and that is something that can help me to make the money to pay the course. (Columbian woman)

> At the moment I am paying my mortgage and I've got kids and it will be very hard for me ... and doing a full-time course. (Venezuelan woman)

> At the moment I am doing some work, I need it because I need to support my family and so it will have to be side by side. (Ghanaian man)

While family responsibilities were not considered a major issue by teachers responding to the survey, some focus group participants raised the possibility of problems arising over how much time they would be expected to give to such a course. All currently worked full time, and needed to be able to work to support their families. The need to work full time while also working in a supplementary school at the weekend would leave them little time for training:

> Because [teachers] work and they don't have time and sometimes you know we have a lot of free training for teachers that come from the council, but the timing is completely ... sometimes it is midday, you know, 1 o'clock and so it is not accommodating for people who work but still want to attend in the evening or the weekend or something like that. And so timing is very important for people working. In my case (Eritrean supplementary school) all the seven teachers we have they work fulltime Monday to Friday ... I wonder also about financial support they know more courses but they need some motivation ... (Eritrean man)

Some focus group participants discussed difficulties related to their UK residency status and whether or not this would prevent them from being able to apply for a course:

> I have been living here for two years. (Columbian woman)

> My visa is like a family [visa]. (Venezuelan woman)

As well as discussing the issues raised in the survey, the focus groups revealed that there was much uncertainty about how to apply for a QTS course and what this would entail. They lacked information about the qualifications they would need and about the matter of UK residency status.

The project team found a lack of awareness of and understanding about routes into teaching other than the PGCE (Postgraduate Certificate). The participants did not know for example, about the GTP (Graduate Teacher Programme) and RTP (Registered Teacher Programme) routes, or that the PGCE could be studied flexibly in a few institutions. As well as misinformation about the costs and the time the course would take, respondents who had not worked as classroom assistants in mainstream schools did not know how to volunteer to become one. One teacher who was interested in special educational needs wondered whether she would have to do a course other than the PGCE to qualify as a special educational needs teacher, and another wondered whether it would be possible to just teach Spanish in a primary school.

Importantly, one teacher wanted to know how a QTS course would differ from the one she had completed on community language teaching, which she considered to be 'like a teacher course':

You know you plan lessons, materials, we learn something different every week. It was like a teacher course. I went there every day, we had the computer, we did everything on the course to be a teacher. It was a very, very good course. (Columbian woman)

Having undertaken such a course, this respondent was of the view that she already had 'the skills to teach' plus competence in the Spanish language.

The Teacher Survey also asked what additional skills teachers thought they might need before beginning a QTS course. The chart below demonstrates that teachers felt there was a need for them to gain additional skills in a number of key areas. The most prominent need was to learn more about the English system of education, with 23 out of 30 teachers agreeing that this was essential.

The need for greater language proficiency was an important skill they thought they would need before embarking on a QTS course. A large proportion (19 teachers) agreed with the statement 'I need to develop my proficiency in English'. But the teachers were understandably more confident about their proficiency in the languages they wished to teach; with half disagreeing that they needed to improve their proficiency.

The need to develop ICT knowledge was also considered necessary; fourteen teachers agreed. So was maths, although to a lesser extent, with a third of teachers agreeing that they needed to improve their maths.

Table 8.6: Additional Skills Needed for QTS

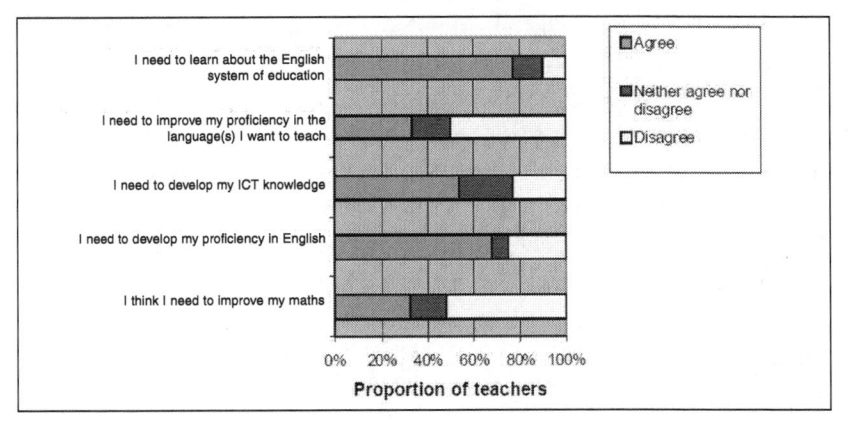

The importance of language proficiency emerges clearly when examining the need for English proficiency against respondents' self-reported proficiency. Whilst eleven teachers identified themselves as 'very fluent' English speakers, just under half (5) agreed that they needed to develop their proficiency; nine out of sixteen who were 'very strong' at reading English agreed and two out of four teachers who were of 'advanced ability' in reading English agreed that they needed to develop their command of English. This was borne out by some of the entries to open questions, some of which revealed weakness in their English.

These possible areas of additional skills were discussed in the focus groups. One of the main difficulties the focus group teachers envisaged if they were to apply for a QTS course, was their level of fluency (written and spoken) in English:

> The main problem when people come from a foreign country, mostly people come from Asia, India and Pakistan especially these two countries you know. What the problem is they have when they come ... still they cannot speak good English. (Pakistani man)

A Latin American teacher described being ridiculed by a group of children when she 'took a lesson' as a teaching assistant. She complained that the children were 'laughing when [she] didn't pronounce a word properly'.

Two of the Latin American teachers had taken a British Council English language qualification in the past three years, one who gained a 'level one certificate' and one at a higher level. Some respondents seemed unaware that there were different English language qualifications (eg IELTS – International English Language Testing System, GCSE grade 'C' or equivalent). They might not have to take GCSEs if their own qualifications are at the right level. They could study in order to gain the required QTS level or that they could have their English language competence tested by the institution to which they applied to study for QTS. Disquiet was expressed by an Indian teacher who considered herself fluent in written and spoken English and had an overseas English language qualification, at the need for overseas-qualified people to have to obtain GCSE English because some overseas qualifications are not recognised:

> I felt really discriminated [against] because they said you have to have a GCSE in English. I've done my engineering in this country what more do you want? I don't want to spend the rest of my life; I'm 43 years old you know, to keep on doing GCSEs and all that. If I was teaching back home but I'm teaching here, and so they are asking all these sorts of questions and they are hindering me. (Indian woman)

All prospective teachers in the UK need such qualifications in English, mathematics and science, but it seems that some supplementary school teachers think that these qualifications are being demanded only of them. Similar concerns were echoed by an Ethiopian head-teacher, who considered the overseas qualification verification process to be discriminatory.

There was also concern lest their mathematics qualifications would not be of the required standard to do a QTS course. One had level 2 GNVQ Maths but was also studying for level 3. One was uncertain as to why a mathematics qualification was needed to teach a community language – 'Why do we need maths? If we are going to teach Spanish, we don't need maths!'

While some respondents worried about their lack of English language qualifications, one teacher wanted to know how someone like herself, with 'lots of experience' but 'no qualifications', could be enabled to become a mainstream teacher. She confessed to not knowing where to start.

As well as maths and English, a few respondents identified the need for developing their ICT skills:

> We have a computer at home and I am able to use it not as an intermediate person. I'm not that excellent but my children are going to school and they are using the computer. (Ghanaian man)

There was general consensus that teachers working in supplementary schools intending to work in mainstream schools would need to develop understanding of the British education system, including policies that are used in schools, the different curriculum areas that are taught, how to plan lessons, understanding different ability levels, how to motivate pupils to learn and develop behaviour management skills. For example:

Like planning lessons: I can handle a class, I've done it a few times. My head she was telling me the other day she said I will watch you with younger kids and I will assess you. I'm quite confident with children,that is no problem at all, the only problem is what to teach. I can teach – I know how to teach but I don't know what to teach. I would like to know more about the curriculum. And so basically I would like to learn that before I start. (Columbian woman)

Another Columbian woman teacher said:

I think maybe understand [how] the system works here and ... it is different culture, different kinds of children and so mainly understanding how it works here, how you catch their attention.

And a woman teacher from Venezuela added:

For me it's a problem because we have different age groups, you can't make a plan according to ability. We have to teach them and that's the problem we have because there is only one group and they are different ages and a different level you know.

Other challenges discussed by the focus group participants included: Actual job opportunities once qualified to teach in mainstream schools; not having access to a school where experience could be gained as a teaching assistant – one teacher recalled waiting 'two years' before being given an opportunity to work as a volunteer at her son's school.

Gaining access to a placement school

An issue arose over community language placements for teachers on the PGCE. Focus group participants raised challenges relating specifically to languages. It was felt that gaining access to appropriate resources might also depend on the language competence of the students being taught in, for instance, Akan/Ga, Somali, Tigrinya or Amharic.

Participants discussed the feasibility of finding a course for teaching community languages and thus securing mainstream employment. It was felt that Spanish speakers would stand a better chance, as schools 'are going to need many [Spanish] teachers to support primary school, many, many teachers' (Columbian woman).

It would be even harder to convince Spanish-speaking teachers that they need to do not only a pre QTS course but also a PGCE:

> We have the language we know very well the language. It is different when it is not your mother tongue, it would be different if I was going to teach English with my accent and I make many mistakes. But with your language you have your language. (Columbian woman)

Another Columbian woman said: 'We studied it at university we did a lot of courses in Columbia'.

Only one of the Columbian teachers accepted that the skills required to teach Spanish to non-Spanish speakers might be different to teaching it as mother tongue:

> I think it is a little different to teach Spanish to people that speak the language for example if you go to the Latin American School you are teaching children that their first language is Spanish. They just need to know grammar and how to write but they speak Spanish. It is different for children that don't speak the language do you understand what I mean? It's different.

Key findings of the CILT report

The data have been largely gathered from a particular sub-set of supplementary school teachers, and cannot be regarded as an overall portrait of the whole group. Data was most easily gathered from teachers in schools where the headteacher has been a willing conduit: teachers and schools interested in engaging with the UK educational mainstream and especially in improving teaching standards.

Teachers who were particularly keen to obtain QTS

For a significant proportion of these teachers the main issue which has emerged in the survey has been obtaining QTS in the UK. A positive correlation was found between these teachers' reasons for wanting QTS to enhance their job prospects and their desire to work in mainstream schools. About four-fifths of the teachers we received questionnaires from had qualifications to degree level (80%) from overseas. Two thirds also had some teaching experience from countries overseas and 37 per cent indicated that they had obtained QTS in the UK.

The different routes into teaching were not widely known: many thought the PGCE was the only option. Only a few of the focus group participants had heard of the Graduate Teacher Programme (GTP), the Registered Teacher Programme (RTP) or the Student Associate Scheme (SAS). Discussion with a group of six Spanish teachers from a Latin

American school and the Director of a supplementary school teacher recruitment agency revealed that none of them were aware of the Overseas Trained Teachers scheme (OTT), although this would be most suitable for them. These teachers only discovered in our focus group that the recruitment agency offered a 'Route to QTS' course, which was followed by school placements organised by the agency.

The teachers had little understanding of the basic qualifications now required of all teachers in the UK, such as GCSE standards in English, mathematics and science, and basic skills standards. Many supplementary school teachers assumed that these requirements were being demanded only of them, in a discriminatory manner.

The teachers described their existing skills and knowledge in languages which ranged from 'modern foreign' to 'community' languages. More than half of the teachers interviewed (52%) indicated that they were qualified to teach languages. A total of 16 languages were noted. Many of these language specialist teachers seek to work in primary schools (43%). The *Primary Languages Framework*, planned to be introduced for KS2 by 2010, might make use of this. The Framework will ensure that all primary schools will introduce a second language, decided by the schools, into the curriculum. The flexibility of the Framework is suited to cater for the delivery of any language in a thematic approach.

These teachers felt they had much to offer mainstream education. Their expertise in languages was often accompanied by maths and science, and some wanted to combine their knowledge of languages with their subject expertise to teach Spanish and science in secondary schools.

Teachers were clear about their own needs. A significant proportion identified proficiency in English, developing their ICT skills and learning about the English/UK education system as being their initial goals before taking on QTS courses. Our focus group discussions showed that these teachers often sought to work in schools as voluntary workers or assistants until they developed the skills required to teach in mainstream schools.

They identified two key challenges to this:

- ▓ establishing initial contact with schools was difficult as they lacked school contacts

■ they admitted lacking the confidence in their spoken English to approach mainstream schools

In Chapter 9 we return to the Complementary Schools Project and discuss our findings. Drawing on the findings of both the London Complementary Schools Project and the CILT report, we end with an exploration of these findings in the context of current educational debates, and our recommendations for the schools and their teachers.

PART FOUR
Findings

9

Evaluation of the London Complementary Schools Project's findings

Language schools

Our data shows that although the main task undertaken by complementary schools for bilingual communities is still the maintenance of community languages, they have other functions too. Some schools are beginning to see their roles as fulfilling a multiplicity of tasks. Instructing children in national curriculum subjects in their community language appeared to foster the learning of both language and subject. Community language instruction was thus taught in a meaningful context. This is in line with the present KS2 *Framework for Languages* which provides a good structure for cross-curricular links in the context of second language learning. The *Framework* promotes a thematic approach to teaching across the curriculum so enabling language learning to be contextualised and made meaningful for pupils.

It was not surprising that the responses to our study came from schools which between them offered instruction in eighteen different languages. The history of these schools might vary but the reasons for setting them up reflect a common vision: to preserve the linguistic and cultural characteristics of their communities. A significant proportion of the responding schools (21.1%) offered both community languages and national curriculum support. This supports our finding in our conversations with teachers and headteachers that they desired to be part of the mainstream and to be complementary rather than supplementary in their ethos and provision.

There are implications for the Department for Children Families and Schools (DCSF): they should support complementary schools both financially and professionally and help them truly to complement children's education. In some boroughs the Ethnic Minority Achievement services (EMA) are taking positive steps to give schools financial support. There are many issues to be considered – for example we found that some of the complementary schools still have to pay fees for using school premises.

A good proportion (15.4%) of responding schools indicated that they offered community language with religious education, and aimed to amalgamate the two. A similar number indicated that they offered three out of four of our sub-categories. This draws attention to the complexity of roles as they move away from the traditional single category of provision.

We found only one school (1.9 per cent) which met Category 6 and offered all four sections of the curriculum. This suggests that the schools are realistic about what they can offer. It may be also have to do with the influence of parents and their views on the ethos of the school. Similarly the fact that no schools offered religious education on its own may be interpreted as a sign of schools moving away from 'religion only' to integrating it into a cross-curricular framework. Some of the schools we visited pointed out that religion should be taught as part of an integrated system: embracing teaching it by linking it to other areas of learning rather than presenting it as a separate subject.

This draws attention to the schools' targets and their realistic expectations about what can be achieved in the time available in a school that operates only at weekends or after schools hours. Not one school offered both NC and RE. The two appear to be incompatible: we found that where RE was central to the school's provision it was for one particular religion, for example Islam. This does not fit with mainstream provision of the subject in the NC, which teaches about six major world faiths. But it is possible that our representative sample simply did not include this particular combination, although we sent questionnaires to over 800 complementary schools.

Only 3.9 per cent (2 out of 52) of schools offered support in the NC only and focused on English, maths and science. Although complementary schools are beginning to extend to national curriculum support, not all are exploiting this to teach community languages through the medium of the heritage language, thus helping their pupils with some of the topics covered in mainstream school. Learning subject content through the community language medium was seen to improve their knowledge of the NC subject while at the same time developing their competence in their community language.

Examining the categories revealed to us just how diverse and complex the schools were. Community language learning was offered to over 500 children in our small sample. This supports our hypothesis that many complementary schools still perceive community language instruction as a powerful way of maintaining community identity.

That there were only two schools which taught the national curriculum supports our point about the status of community language instruction. But it also signals a need for initiatives to explore forming closer links between the two. Many schools still perceive their main role as supporting the community language but accept that relating it to NC subjects can enhance pupils' learning. They feel that establishing stronger links with the mainstream schools would optimise provision.

There are also issues about the availability of qualified staff and the training of the complementary schoolteachers to bridge the gap between the two sectors. More important, however, is the role of the local education authorities in facilitating such training – a matter we discuss in our concluding chapter. However, the responses received from complementary schools which have staff who are trained to teach the NC are positive. In the schools we visited, links established between NC and community language instruction appeared to be benefiting the pupils' learning. As a 13 year old girl told us, it was 'more fun this way'. She said it helped her to understand 'some of missing bits of science in my other school and helped my Turkish as well' (Ayla, aged 13).

We noted that using the community language to teach the school curriculum worked in established complementary schools which had staff qualified in their country of origin, often graduates in core NC subjects.

Although the styles of teaching might be different in mainstream and community schools, lesson content is similar. It was observed that the medium of instruction in the community language created interest and even amusement among the pupils and this compensated for the teachers' somewhat didactic approach. However, a number of teachers described to us how having appropriate training in the UK helped change them to adopt more child centred approaches. As they said:

> Before the course I used to think the method I was using was the best one. I can see why see why I am getting better results with a different approach. The training really helped (Mrs. Ahmed, Turkish school)

> I definitely think training at the Resource Unit made a difference to my teaching (Mr. Dhillon, Panjabi School)

> Children here are different. They need a number of approaches, not just one. The training on learning styles really helped me see this (Mr. Hussein, Iraqi School)

Offering national curriculum support appeared to attract more pupils to a community school. Clearly, the parents were concerned about their children's achievement and school learning. Many parents told us that the 'dual functionality' of the schools made learning much more meaningful for their children and improved their understanding of lessons in their 'English' schools. Parents we spoke to indicated that their children benefited from additional English lessons and in some cases were motivated to learn the community language too.

> I need to be honest and say that the main reason why I brought my daughter here was because of extra support in Maths, Science and English. We are all from Gujarati background but we always spoke English at home. Two weeks ago she came home and asked me what was for dinner in Gujarati. I must say I was pleasantly surprised' (Mrs. Bakshi, Gujarati School)

But in the other schools where the community language and RE were offered in tandem, learning Arabic was synonymous with learning about Islam. In one particular category of Islamic school, Arabic was seen essentially as a language of grammar, phonology and semantics. The teachers perceived Arabic as much more than a language: it was the tool through which the essentials of Islam were to be transmitted. Language was embedded in cultural and religious practice. Reciting verses from the Qu'ran was seen as fulfilling the religious functions of the school while also teaching children to be literate in the language of Islam. What is debatable is whether this can be perceived as community language instruction for pupils who do not have Arabic as their community language. What was lacking was the awareness of some senior staff in these schools of the important link between community language and the development of the child's second language, when this was not always Arabic:

> Here we teach about Islam and Arabic is the language of Islam. We are aware that Arabic is not the first language of some of our children but I think in view of the ethos of our school for them learning in Arabic has to be paramount (Headteacher, Arabic school)

In other schools religious education was delivered as a communal event. Children were given guidance on moral issues that related to particular aspects of Islam. RE often took the form of the celebration of important religious events, which were shared during school assemblies. The language used for religious teaching varied. In cases where the language of the religion differed from the children's community languages, such as for Gujerati or Tamil speakers, this was compensated for by instruction in their community language and 'religious language' was essentially used to teach particular aspects of the religion eg teaching the five pillars of Islam. Here, Arabic was used as the language of those who shared a common faith and incorporated distinctly Islamic/Arabic vocabulary such as *zekât* (distribution of one fortieth of one's income as alms according to the faith). One of the teachers in the school pointed to the 'unifying' role of Arabic as the language of Islam:

> We use Arabic when we are teaching about Islam but we also have children who are from Islamic backgrounds but speak other languages so we employ staff that teach those languages. So they come together when they are learning about Islam as well as other religions. We use Arabic in the lessons then. For the second part of the morning they go in their language groups. We feel this is important when we are bringing up children in a multicultural environment. Here Arabic is used as a unifying and an instructional capacity (Senior teacher, Arabic School)

The schools that offered three curricula tended to provide a combination of community language, national curriculum and Religious Education. CL and NC were closely linked in some schools, while in others the curriculum was offered separately in homework classes, or GCSEs were taught in the NC core subjects of maths, science or English. When we looked at the reasons for offering three different curricula it seemed to relate to parental choice. Most parents were very involved in the complementary schools. In almost all those we visited, parents worked as volunteers, helping in the classrooms or serving on the executive group which made decisions. One parent describes her commitment:

> ...doing my bit really. We are aware that our school would not survive without our help. The local authority only visits us when there is a local election pouring out loads of empty promises. We need to be involved. My son learns Somali because it is important to us. I feel I am being useful. I also serve on the committee, which means I have a say in how my son is educated. It is a communal thing. We are like a family here (Parent, Somali School)

We found the CL and NC combination worked best when the teachers had put clear planning and evaluation systems in place. Such schools often used the latter part of Saturday afternoons to go through work and evaluate their teaching approaches. Some of the teachers we interviewed were graduates in maths and science and had professional qualifications from their country of origin. We found evidence of knowledge and skills relating to the NC generally as well as in a particular NC subject.

> I graduated from a Colombian University with a Science Degree. I taught in secondary schools there for five years. Here I find that the NC Science is not much different from ours. Even the terminology is the same. I just need to work on the pronunciation (Teacher, Spanish School)

> I attended a training course on the British Education System at the Resource Centre. I hold a Maths degree from Bangladesh. It made me realise that NC is not as difficult as some people make it out to be (Teacher, Bengali School)

Only one school offered all four types of curriculum. It is therefore difficult to predict whether this indicates the emergence of a new category of schools designed to fulfil the multiplicity of education requirements in complex multicultural settings, or whether it is unique, created to meet the special arrangements of a particular community in the UK, in this case the Cabindan/Angolan Congolese school we visited. The school's co-ordinator Jose Lebina told us that the relatively high staff-pupil ratio (7:20) plus the availability of appropriately trained staff enabled them to deliver all the different curricula. The school boasted seven teachers, two UK trained and five with overseas qualifications, plus three volunteers. It operates in the building used as an advice centre for the community. It was explained to us that the location increased the chances of daily contact with parents and was useful for recruiting volunteers.

> The school developed out of the advice centre which we have set up for the community. We started with basic resources and one full time staff member trying to meet ever increasing need of the members of the community. These families had children. Our need to set up the school grew out of the desire expressed by the parents to teach their children French, Lingala or Kikongo here. (Jose Lebina, Centre manager)

Evaluation of the African Caribbean Complementary schools

Evidence from our data indicate that African Caribbean complementary schools today still uphold the principles articulated by Bernard Coard in 1971 and instituted by the pioneers of supplementary education in the late 1960s through to the 1980s. Jessica and Eric Huntley in west London, John La Rose in north London, Gloria Cameron, Ansel Wong and Gerlin Bean in south London, Gus John in Manchester and Lola Young in Leeds are but a distinguished few of those who took up the challenge of improving the educational opportunities of black children.

Today people in the African and Caribbean communities continue to responded to Coard's call to construct 'the best armour against the prejudice and humiliating experiences many black children still face'. Three generations on, after numerous government enquiries and reports on the crisis of black children's education – Rampton (1981), Swann (1985) and Macdonald (1989) – funding and the initiatives of Section 11, then the Ethnic Minority Achievement Grant black children are still short changed in the British education system. A Priority Review by the government in 2006 which investigated the disproportionate number of black children being excluded from school states:

> ... discrimination against the grandchildren and great grandchildren of the early Black migrants persists in the form of culturally unrepresentative curricula and low expectations for attainment and behaviour on the part of staff. Many argue that the disparity in exclusion rates for Black pupils (the 'exclu-

sions gap') is a modern manifestation of the same process that saw so many Black pupils classified as 'Educationally Sub-Normal' in the past. (Wanless, 2006)

Recent research by Steve Strand of Warwick University echoes the Wanless Review (2006) in explicitly naming institutional racism as contributing to the underachievement of black children (*Education Guardian*, September 5 2008).

Getting it. Getting it Right (DfES, 2007) recognises racism – institutional racism – as a factor in the structuring of relationships between pupils and teachers that results in disproportionally damaging outcomes for black pupils, especially boys. 'Black Caribbean pupils', it states, 'are three times more likely to be excluded from school than White pupils'. It goes on: 'In fact since 2000, the proportion of Black pupils excluded has increased, and more rapidly, than for any other group' (Wanless, 2006: 8-10).

Bernard Coard reviewed the situation for black children in Britain in 2005 when his seminal booklet of 1971 was republished, along with chapters by modern activists and academics. He advocated that:

> We should start up supplementary schools in whatever part of London, or Britain, we live, in order to give our children additional help in the subject they need. These classes can be held on evenings and Saturday mornings. We should recruit all our Black students and teachers for the task of instructing our children. Through these schools we hope to make up for the inadequacies of the British school system and for its refusal to teach our children our history and culture. (Coard in Richardson, 2005:52)

In 1971, Coard was calling attention to the disproportionate numbers of black children wrongly tested and allocated to educationally subnormal schools. Discriminatory educational practice continues today most strikingly in the form of exclusions from school. Chris Searle is right to stress the relevance of Coard's work to the education crisis black children still face in the twenty-first century:

> His [Coard's] concluding section *Things we can do for ourselves* is as relevant now as it was in 1971. Similarly, with a few words changes, his five introductory points are still absolutely key to the contemporary struggle against Black exclusions from school. 'There are very large numbers of our West Indian children being excluded from school. These children have been

wrongly excluded. Once excluded from these schools, the vast majority never regain their place in mainstream schools. They suffer academically and in their job prospects for life because of being put out of these schools. The authorities are doing very little to stop this scandal.' (2006:62-63)

The education crisis for black children persists and the black communities continue to resist this mass branding of its children as 'academic underachievers' by organising complementary schools.

A number of complementary schools in our surveys reported that they began their schools in response to the failure of state schools to educate African Caribbean children successfully and the growing demands of parents who wanted to help their children's academic advancement. Olive complementary school, for instance, wrote that it was started in order 'to address the underachievement of African Caribbean children and to improve pupils' academic performance'.

Three others, Amy, Progressive and Youth, reported that they started as a direct response to parental concerns and persistent requests for additional schooling for their children. Progressive wrote that the '...pressing need for additional education support expressed by parents and the need to bridge the visible gaps in children's education' motivated the establishing of their school. Some schools, such as Blacks, Marcus, Kaye and Roots, were initially set up by parents as a response to their children's poor educational achievement and mainstream school teachers' negative attitudes towards their children. Parents remain central to the ongoing organisation and running of complementary schools. I return to this point below.

By responding to the educational crisis of African Caribbean children, all the schools in this survey sought to provide a curriculum that addressed the mis-education of black children and declared similar intentions in their literature and communication with the community. One of them, Olive, stated that it aimed to

- improve pupils' academic performance
- develop the positive self image of pupils
- help pupils develop greater confidence in their abilities
- make learning stimulating and worthwhile
- promote black history and culture

Yam declared its mission as being to 'promote learning and community cohesion within the African community'. Africa recorded their aim to 'assist children aged 5-11 in their curriculum work'. Treasure was motivated by 'various surveys (that) showed that African/Caribbeans were underachieving', and these acted as the catalyst for starting up their school.

The majority of respondents recognised the political climate in which the schools are established and operating, and acknowledge that the schools are the response to ineffective government policies and an education system that continues to fail black children and their parents. Complementary schools acknowledge that they have to compensate for the failures of state education. A few schools who did not explicitly espouse a political position nonetheless demonstrated their acquiescence to an Afrocentric education philosophy. Schools like Baddish, Roots, Progressive and Unity call for a culturally relevant curriculum and identify 'ethnicity' as a factor that operates in mainstream schools to undermine and destroy African Caribbean children's enthusiasm and motivation to learn. Their mission was therefore to empower black children to achieve their academic potential. Progressive's headteacher reflected the philosophy of all the schools when she gave her reasons for starting the school as: to 'help to bridge visible gaps in children's learning and to build children's self esteem and develop their untapped potential'.

Also significant in developing and implementing an Afrocentric philosophy was using resources within the curriculum that reflected black culture and identity. The presence of black adults as human resources was considered an important aspect of this process. Coard (2005) had in his recent essay stipulated the need to have...

> resources such as black dolls and toys, pictures and storybooks about great black men and women and their achievements and inventions. Such resources are necessary to help support and develop children's academic skills as well as nurture their psychological and cultural understanding of themselves and their communities. The transmission of cultural knowledge is important, to stop children being made into 'ignoramuses'. (Coard, 2005:52)

African and Caribbean traditions and cultural values were explicitly promoted and taught in some schools, one school reflecting in its name the centrality of culture to its function. Yet culturally related resources were not very evident when we visited. The children appeared to bring their own work books and pencils to school. The most striking feature of the data we collected showed that complementary schools were, however, well equipped with human resources. The majority of teachers were drawn from black communities. The schools reflected the ethnicity of the communities in which they are located.

All the teachers were qualified, most having gained qualified teacher status (QTS) in Britain, as well as holding teaching qualifications from countries overseas. Only one school had a teacher with teaching qualifications but no QTS. The qualifications, experience and motivation of the teachers was frequently stressed in a school's literature and was also one of the questions posed in our questionnaire. Because they reflect the communities they come from, complementary school teachers are sometimes mistakenly perceived as lacking formally recognised qualifications. This stereotypical view of these teachers could help to explain why the complementary schools ensure that they signal the qualifications of their teaching staff clearly. The teachers' qualifications were very apparent in our data: over 70 of the teachers from the eighteen schools were UK qualified, with an additional eleven holding an overseas teaching qualification.

Kaye's brochure declared that, '...teaching is provided in a supportive environment by qualified teachers in core National Curriculum subjects up to GCSE level'. Olive school wrote out the National Curriculum stages its teachers catered for, plus the credentials of the teachers it recruits:

We aim to:

- improve the pupils' academic performance by providing tuition in English, Maths, Science and French
- prepare pupils for KS1, KS2 KS3 and GCSE
- recruit the services of qualified teachers from the African/Caribbean community to teach and assist in the promotion of positive self image.

Yam pointed out that five of its seven teaching staff held both overseas and UK teaching qualifications.

Another factor emerged from our data as contributing significantly to the success of the education which complementary schools provide: the ratio of children to qualified teachers. Our figures showed a ratio of 13:1. Such a favourable ratio gives children significant advantage compared with the mainstream school which could be operating in classes with ratios of 26:1 through to 30:1. This teaching ratio became even more favourable (11:1) if we added in the volunteers.

Complementary school teachers recognised the value of small teaching groups and remark on how this factor contributes to the success of children's learning. When asked what it is they most liked most about teaching in their schools, teachers from Youth, Treasure, Progressive, Blacks and Roots all commented on the fact that small teaching groups lead to student success. A teacher from Baddish summed it up as follows:

> The one to one relationship gives the children the confidence they need to tackle work in which they may have previously failed.

Progressive goes further, insisting on small groups as they see this approach as a criterion for success. The Team leader wrote that:

> Progressive insists on small group sizes, in order to provide an appropriate and stimulating learning experience in pursuit of the desired results of parents, students and the wider community.

Pedagogy

A prerequisite for the self help education operating in African Caribbean communities was that consideration be given to the taught curriculum as well as to the emotional and psychological needs of black children. Coard stipulated that all these features be considered in constructing any agenda for teaching and learning. In 2005, he reflected that:

> Our children need to have a sense of identity, pride and belonging as well as mental stimulation so that they do not end up hating themselves and their race. (Coard, 2005:52).

Therefore if black children are to become successful motivated learners, the taught curriculum needs to encompass teaching them about themselves and about the 'good and the great' from their communities. All the schools in our survey taught the core national curriculum subjects, English, maths and science and some also teach ICT. Black history and geography form part of the taught and social curriculum and several schools taught African and Caribbean traditional dance/drama. Four schools taught French, reflecting the composition of French African Caribbean speakers in their communities. One multilingual African school enabled its children to successfully access the NC in the language of the community and used a third language, Arabic, for religious instruction. The then Minister of Schools implied that schools such as this one should consider becoming a specialist Language school under the remit of the Labour Government (Adonis, 2006).

In the schools we visited, dialects and community languages, while not exclusively the language of instruction, are widely used in classes, for teaching and general communication with children and parents. A good example of the integrated curriculum appears in Kaye's brochure:

> Kaye prides itself in providing tuition which enhances the student's attainment in their National Curriculum studies. However, the organisation recognises the importance of integrating the African and African-Caribbean cultural and historical perspectives into the work of the school.

The teachers' comments about their schools and the work they do on Saturdays conveyed their collective desire to arrest the failure of mainstream schooling and to re motivate and 'nurture' children back into becoming active and excited learners. The teachers were proud and confident about their schools. One wrote: 'The main strength is having qualified, experienced tutors who share their different experiences in order to meet the varied needs of the children'.

Commenting on the children's ability, another teacher wrote that what she liked most about her class was 'their enthusiasm and eagerness to learn, [and] watching the less confident blossom over the year'. A teacher at Progressive who felt well supported and that her experience was validated by the team, wrote about her pleasure at 'seeing the children overcome their worries, gain confidence in their own ability and realise that they can and *do* achieve'. She went on: 'seeing them present their work to parents, friends and other pupils with confidence and panache is a great joy!'

One parent commented on the quality of the facilities in the school setting attended by her child. It offered five subjects, including drama, which gave pupils exposure to a regular theatre group. She said that her school had 'created an environment that encourages learning and a sense of fun'.

The impression gained from the teachers' responses to our questions about the strengths of their schools and what the school was doing well was very informative. They demonstrate their knowledge of the children they teach, and their academic abilities. Consequently they can provide work at an appropriately challenging level, thus supporting and motivating children's learning. The smaller class sizes, combined with close working relationships with the parents, also contributed to the successful learning of the children.

Black parents and teachers

Parents were instrumental in starting the Black Parents Education Movement and many Saturday schools started in 'somebody's front room' (John, 2006; Mirza and Reay, 1996) and later moved out to church halls and community centres as pupil numbers grew through word of mouth. Today African Caribbean complementary schools operate in community centres, libraries, youth clubs and mainstream school buildings as well as in their own rented or leased premises.

African Caribbean complementary schools are predominantly, although not exclusively, staffed and managed by women. However our data revealed a gender shift in participation and provided a snapshot of changing gender relations. The schools have become similar to the current hierarchies in mainstream education, with male teachers acquiring managerial positions as schools become larger and more established. Half the respondents to our survey identified themselves as directors, lead teachers and team leaders and half of these were women. But among those who identified themselves as teachers or volunteers, women outnumbered male teachers by approximately four to one. This was the case in seven schools we visited over the course of the project. Five of the lead women teachers were instrumental in setting up and running their school, as were two men – all of them parents of children attending the school.

Reay and Mirza (1996) talk of the 'awe-inspiring black women' they interviewed for their research project and observed that these women 'tell tales of effective Black agency' for African Caribbean communities. In their study:

> All four schools had been set up primarily by women. If supplementary schooling is a new social movement it certainly is not one led predominantly by men ... Carol, who had worked as a full time coordinator at (name of school) was adamant: 'It's mainly women who are the ones who are involved in education in this country. Within the Afro-Caribbean community it tends to be a mainly women. In my family that was the case and at ... it was mainly women who came and that was fine. Obviously, there are a few fathers who were involved and there were a couple of men who were on the committee but it was mainly women. (1996:1)

David Simon, who opened Ebony Supplementary Saturday School in east London in 1987, also pays tribute to the dedication and fortitude of women with in the supplementary school movement and acknowledges that:

> The supplementary school movement has been largely built by women – teachers, mothers and volunteers. An area that requires further investigation is that of the many women and men who have dedicated themselves to complementing black children's education. A job that involves much more than teaching; for many it is a second job. These teachers have a long working week planning, teaching and working with children [and] communicating with parents. They also have to organise timetables, manage their school; interact with local education agencies, authorities, trusts, and charities, advocate on behalf of children and parents and much, much more, for little or no remuneration. (Simon, 2005:69)

The biographies of black educators need to be better known and validated. Gus John (2006) claims that supplementary school teachers provide the finest example of teachers preparing and equipping 'school students and parents with appropriate strategies for surviving in mainstream schools and breaking the cycle of low expectations, high order frustration, and poor educational outcome' (p123) and we observed this in our research (see also Aubrey's story on page 68).

Business, fees and funding

Increased recognition of the role complementary schools play in education provision and the Local Management of Schools regulations (LMS) has caused some authorities and Trusts to provide some limited financial assistance to schools, as well as facilitating setting up support networking within their authorities. The Director of Hackney Young People and Community wrote in the forward to Hackney Supplementary Schools Directory:

> ... The establishment of the supplementary School Forum puts us all in a strong and united position to work together, which will enable us to move forward with the Government's aims of having supplementary education playing a major role in the advancement and increased attainment for young people and students of African Caribbean and Turkish ethnicity'. (2007)

The government envisaged supplementary schools as intersecting with one of three national policy programmes through which they could get funding: the extended schools, specialist schools or the teaching and learning of languages programme. The Schools Minister advised that it is in the extended schools programme that African Caribbean organisations or partners can best participate. He wrote:

> ... all good supplementary schools add to the work of mainstream schools; some of them – such as those engaging with under motivated or disaffected pupils – make a valuable contribution in this respect ... African Caribbean supplementary schools could be housed in local schools, a feature that already existed amongst some authorities'. (Andrew Adonis in *Education Guardian* 26 April, 2006)

Several of our respondents observed that their relationship with education authorities was key to the management of their schools. One called for more dialogue and involvement with the funding bodies. Another CS manager observed that funding agencies need to reward success and longevity and, when asked what would help to resolve funding issues, replied: 'the preparedness of grant-making trusts to support proven success. All too often they just support new ventures' (Baddish).

A third CS manager made the point that funding needed to be reasonable, and that funders should not seek to use their financial leverage to assert unreasonable control over the school. A school which was particularly critical of funding arrangements claimed that the authority simply wanted cheap labour.

Complementary schools have various financial arrangements. A few ask for donations; others have annual fees with a sliding scale, depending on the number of children attending from one family. Still others have set up trust funds or 'sponsor a child' programmes, and some have attained charitable status to sustain their financial independence. It appeared that relationships with education authorities were mainly centred around funding. We cannot tell from our data how many of our respondents are funded by Education Trusts or local government.

Our concluding observations on black schools

Certain positive factors emerged from our study, notably

- a curriculum that reflects children's and the communities' experiences
- leadership by teachers who are knowledgeable about the ambitions and aspirations of the community.
- experienced and qualified teachers
- small teaching groups

Complementary schools can engender positive aspirations in black children and counter the stereotype of their being underachievers. As one parent said about her child after he had attended Progressive complementary school for a few weeks: '...They come here and they learn!'

African Caribbean complementary schools, with their favourable staffing ratios, high parental participation and their active engagement with the community's academic expectations, ambitions, hopes, aspirations and attitudes exemplifies Bourdieu's (1986) construction of *habitus* which, he asserts, gives rise to the creation of valuable 'cultural capital'. Is this what is going on in African Caribbean complementary schools? Callender (1997) offers us insights into the value of shared cultural knowledge. She explored the *simpatico* relationships that exist between teachers and children sharing the same cultural norms and thus the shared cultural knowledge of *habitus*. Callender's study explored how teachers put their shared cultural knowledge and understanding of language to good use, and how they used gestures and facial expressions to interact and keep their pupils engaged with learning. Teachers, she argued, are part of the children's community and share the community aspirations. So they use their cultural knowledge to inform their relationships with and expectations of the children they teach.

This chapter highlights the importance of complementary schools and shows that those studied were dynamic and successful institutions. It shows how black complementary schools and those set up to teach languages all developed know-how and successful classroom strategies to enable ethnic minority children to become successful learners. What emerged above all is the need for more collaboration with the mainstream schools.

The findings of the London Complementary Schools Project and the CILT report reinforce one another and underpin our recommendations in the final chapters of this book. These recommendations concern teachers and pupils in all complementary schools but also have profound implications for maintained schools and the education system as a whole.

10

Conclusions and Recommendations

The picture of complementary schools that emerges in this book is of dynamic institutions which contribute significantly to children's academic achievement, and of able, committed and generally well qualified staff. More could be done, however, to realise the full potential of both teachers and pupils and this book seeks to identify what needs to be done.

Our picture is of two main providers that serve the diverse needs of minority communities: black complementary schools and language schools. We found that a significant majority of these schools have moved away from their traditionally ascribed roles to respond to the needs of their communities. A significant proportion of the schools that responded to our questionnaires offered support in the national curriculum, religious education and the history and culture of the ethnic groups the school served. We found that schools offered different combinations of the subcategories we identified rather than aiming to provide support in every way.

We had one particular interest: what contribution do complementary schools make to the academic achievement of black and bilingual children in mainstream schooling?

In the schools we visited we met many enthusiastic and hard working students who told us they were proud of their identity. Jerome aged 13, summed it up:

We are learning about our language and culture and we are also part of this country. We have best of both worlds. (French School)

There is ample evidence, however, that complementary schools are also enhancing children's self esteem. There is virtually no empirical evidence but we believe that qualitative and anecdotal evidence we have set out here is a valuable beginning.

Our other major finding was the significant amount of support the schools give to the learning of the national curriculum through teaching the subjects using the pupils' languages. We observed this approach to be particularly effective when a NC subject was taught through a community language. Sometimes the pedagogy was overly traditional but we mostly observed child centred, interactive and well planned activities in the classrooms. Some of these were especially impressive in light of the time constraints on lesson preparation and the limited resources most of the teachers had access to.

During our interviews with headteachers and parents, one of the major issues that came up was about training. Every person we spoke to agreed that the government needed to take a more active role in providing training for complementary school teachers. Understanding the British education system and familiarity with government legislation came top of the training priorities they mentioned.

We found ample evidence of the government's support for complementary schools. The latest move to partly fund the National Resource Centre for Supplementary Schools is a step in the right direction but clearly this is not enough. Our study revealed how many schools are struggling to cope with the cost of running their schools. Many complementary schools hired mainstream school premises to run classes on Saturdays or as after-school clubs on weekdays. All of them relied on contributions from parents and struggled to pay their way.

A recent meeting organised by the National Resource Centre for complementary school managers and head teachers set out to decide what key points should to be raised with the Minister for Schools in advance of the scheduled meeting with him. One of the major issues for discussion concerned the difficulties over paying rent for schools premises. Mr. Çakıcı, the head teacher of Hornsey Atatürk School, summed up their difficulties:

We have been running our school for 25 years. We use the premises of a local secondary school. We pay £500.00 for every three hours. We only have money that comes in from parental contributions. In order for the school to survive I have been trying to meet the schools' rental costs. When I started this work I had three businesses. Now I have one and I am running on my bank's overdraft limit.

In chapter 1 we described the social and political factors that drove the formation of complementary schools. We showed how migration and settlement patterns necessitated community support and cohesion. To a newcomer, Britain was a strange and a hostile place. Being with members of the same community usually presented a fairly secure environment to set oneself up for work until things got better. Some moved on but others stayed. Communities grew as more newcomers arrived and a second generation was born. Setting up community schools and drawing on the skills and resources of one's own community in order to maintain one's cultural and linguistic identity offered some protection against racism.

Similar conditions existed for African and African Caribbean schools. Disaffection with the education system that so often labelled black children as 'educationally subnormal' brought together community activists, teachers and parents, who set up schools to compensate for the damage and miseducation of black children. This led to the creation of the Black Parents Movement and the complementary school movement spread to areas where sizable numbers of the black population had settled. The curriculum and the ethos of complementary schools helped to restore black children's self esteem and confidence as learners.

Chapter 2 described the current provision in complementary schools. Since the Swann Report of 1985, the Conservative government had shifted its position and although it declared its support for complementary schools, this was little more than lipservice. However, recently the government offered financial assistance to CILT, the National Centre for Languages, to conduct research into complementary school teachers' professional aspirations and the barriers they encountered (CILT, 2008). The DCSF is supporting the National Resource Centre for Supplementary Schools' training programmes for complementary school teachers. Both are significant steps in the right direction. These programmes, although not directly leading to educational qualifications, may support the teachers when they apply for accredited courses.

But complementary schools face such serious financial difficulties that even these initiatives are clearly not enough. We found some schools that operate on Saturdays used all their funds to hire school premises and had hardly any resources. We discovered that many mainstream schools did not share their resources with the complementary schools, locking away their materials on Friday afternoons. Some LAs did try to provide funding for their complementary schools but could only help a few as their own budgets were inadequate. Different LAs used different criteria for funding local complementary schools but one of the criteria we noted was the number of pupils attending each school.

Parents are the schools' main source of funding, except in the case of some African Caribbean schools which are funded mainly by the Church. Understandably the Church then has a say in the running of the school and was represented on the management committee. A few schools have become Trusts, and obtained charity status and set up a Trustees' committee made up of the headteacher, a teacher representative and other elected parents. Management committees are responsible for overseeing the delivery of the school curriculum, recruitment of staff, deciding the teachers' pay and the school fees. Some schools employed teachers who are contracted by the relevant embassies. Each year parents elect the Executive Committee democratically. In most cases we found complementary schools functioning as self-sufficient and independent institutions.

Recommendations of the CILT Report

The following recommendations are addressed to CILT but the project team recognise that in order to implement them CILT will need to work with a range of other organisations, for example the National Resource Centre for Supplementary Education and the teacher training and recruitment consultants, Empowering Learning. It would need to enter into discussions with Ofsted, the TDA and the DCSF about how these proposals can be implemented.

■ For a significant proportion of teachers the main issue is obtaining QTS in order to teach in mainstream schools in the UK. Teachers were often given conflicting advice and stayed on some courses much longer than was required, unnecessarily prolonging the process. There need to be joint programmes between all parties – the schools and LAs, with support and advice from local and national organisations – to provide training and advice for complementary school teachers. There are agencies which already undertake this work and the expertise within them can be used to support such initiatives.

- The CILT study shows the need for a pre-QTS course which would provide the appropriate skills and information to complementary school teachers wishing to qualify to teach in mainstream schools. Teachers the project team have interviewed indicated that they would benefit from receiving input in the following areas:

  - □ advice on the routes into teaching other than the PGCE, for example GTP, RTP, OTT (virtually all respondents appeared to need this)

  - □ knowledge of the British education system (95%)

  - □ knowledge in ICT (78%)

  - □ improving skills in English language (75%), maths (48%) and science

  - □ developing skills in teaching community languages

- The CILT study and our own indicate that many teachers would need funding, for example in the form of a bursary, to help support them so they could participate in a course of this kind.

- There needs to be a concerted effort to channel cases through professional organisations that assess each applicant's needs individually, and thence to suitable training paths to obtaining QTS. Agencies such as CILT, The National Resource Centre and Empowering Learning are already undertaking work in this area and provide effective models.

- There was widespread recognition among supplementary school teachers of the dearth of opportunities to teach their community languages in mainstream schools. Some teachers expressed their desire to combine their knowledge of languages with their subject expertise in national curriculum subjects. For example, 61 per cent expressed their willingness to teach mathematics while 64 per cent indicated that they would be happy to teach languages. In some secondary schools with a significant number of ethnic minority children, community languages are not being offered. The teachers' expertise could be used to children's advantage by offering not only the language but also support in a national curriculum subject. The team recognise that teachers will need some training before this could be realised effectively. The role of LAs is crucial in identifying and advising schools accordingly.

■ The headteachers of the CSs identified funding and resources as the two key issues determining their ability to retain their teachers. National as well as local initiatives are required to provide financial assistance to supplementary schools.

■ The Report findings point to the need for research across regional locations to gain a fuller understanding about the needs and aspirations of supplementary teachers wishing to work in mainstream schools. The project teams believe that there will probably be significant regional variations and that these should be explored. It would be useful to approach a wider range of supplementary schools than could be accessed in a London based study such as the CILT project and it is recommended that provision in other cities be explored.

Teaching NC subjects in community languages

Although community language teaching is still provided in almost all of the complementary schools serving linguistic minorities, we found that the focus was changing to incorporate national curriculum subjects. This gave the schools a dual purpose. The parents' educational aspirations for their children's achievement and their recognition of the new role of the complementary schools in enabling their children's learning in the mainstream appear to be driving this change.

The role of community languages has been hotly debated for decades. The need for such debate has arisen out of the communities' concerns about

- ■ the level of underachievement of their children in mainstream education and

- ■ issues relating to the teaching of community languages

There appeared to be a rational justification for change, at least superficially. The real concern was over the *content* of what was to be taught. Teachers often used imported resources (mainly textbooks and storybooks) featuring topics which had no relevance to the experiences of children born in the UK. Production of appropriate UK based materials looked like a good option but soon had to be abandoned because of the lack of time and funding. This prompted parents and community educators to consider the merits of a possible link between the community language and the English national curriculum.

Clearly this presented its own challenges. Too few of the bilingual teachers who taught in complementary schools were trained in the UK and this remains a challenge today. Our survey showed that the curriculum was taught mostly by specialist teachers of the subject (mainly maths and science) who had graduated overseas. These teachers used their own initiative, attending short inservice training programmes to develop their knowledge of English to deliver key components of the NC subjects through their community language. We found this approach to be one of the success stories of complementary schools today. Marked increases in student numbers were recorded in schools where such provision was offered.

We found that the complementary schoolteachers demonstrated their high aspirations for their pupils' future by positively addressing the issue of training. In the sample of schools we visited, we found much excellent practice despite the challenges they faced. Although some teachers used traditional approaches, children in almost all the classes were given plenty of opportunities to develop literacy skills in both their languages. The content of teaching, especially in NC subjects, was similar to units used in mainstream schools. It was refreshing to see children expressing their satisfaction in having recognisably similar units delivered through their home languages.

Other subjects were taught too. Religious education was taught not as a separate subject but integrated into other areas such as social studies or topic work and explored faith in the context of all religions while supporting the pupils' own cultural or linguistic development. Most schools offered extracurricular activities in the afternoon, giving children the chance to learn folk dancing, play an instrument or take part in drama activities relating to their cultural identity.

The professional aspirations of complementary school teachers

A significant number of teachers we interviewed said they would like to work in mainstreams schools. We discovered that most of them had degrees from overseas, generally in languages. Those who were not language graduates had developed their expertise in teaching their home languages through working in complementary schools. In some cases we found issues with regard to pedagogy but the teachers' knowledge of their subjects was evident from what they told us, and what we observed of their lessons.

Our findings about the educational aspirations of the complementary school teachers and the barriers they faced were supported by the CILT commissioned research (CILT, 2008) (see Chapters 6 and 7). Overall, the report revealed vibrant, enthusiastic and committed teachers in the complementary school, eager to contribute to teaching languages and national curriculum subjects in mainstream schools. The CILT findings resonate with our own: the schools continue to maintain their strong community links, serving the diverse needs of the communities. The CILT report's findings also echoed our finding that in most schools traditional 'community languages only' policies were changing to include support in national curriculum subjects, mainly in mathematics, science and English. We think the changing and complex roles of complementary schools are significant and that they have implications for mainstream schools.

The ongoing importance of black complementary schools

Aubrey's story (see page 68) illustrates that complementary schools have a healthy future in the black communities. *Tell It Like It Is: how our schools fail Black children,* with its republication of Bernard Coard's seminal book (Richardson, 2005) plus recent commentaries by academics and activists, shows that racial discrimination against black pupils still persists. Because ethnic minority communities and parents continue to struggle against racism, complementary schools remain vibrant and active locations of struggle against racism in education.

The indicators from our research project concur with our professional knowledge of good education practice, and reflect the success criteria published by Ofsted in 2005. They echo the proposals published in successive governments' reports dating back as far as the Rampton Report (1981) and more recently in the Priority Review *Getting it. Getting it right* (Wanless, 2007). Our research did not set out to investigate racism, but rather to explore an area of community action that began in the late 1960s as a response to institutionalised racism. Complementary schools set out to compensate for what Macpherson (1999) describes as 'the collective failure of the education system'.

In the government review on the exclusion of black pupils, Wanless acknowledges and strives to incorporate black parents' knowledge and experience of racism in education. He writes:

> Traditionally, exclusion has been the yardstick by which Black communities have judged the successes (or failure) of the education system. Whilst Black commentators are often keen to stress that the exclusion gap is the tip of an iceberg – a symptom of widespread discrimination through the system – they have highlighted it as an iconic issue. For Black communities, exclusions are to education what stop-and-search is to criminal justice. (2007:14)

Exclusions are indeed the tip of the education iceberg of racism, and it is often complementary schools that provide a protective and supportive environment for the children from the minority communities. Wanless provides an endorsement of the response of black and ethnic minority communities in establishing alternative and complementary schooling opportunities for their children.

The success of complementary schools, as highlighted in our small investigation, indicates certain models of good classroom practice from which mainstream schools could learn. Complementary schools are organic to their communities. Teachers and parents share a understanding of racism. Being themselves part of ethnic minority communities, the teachers are uniquely placed to know how racism operates in schools and how children and their parents experience it.

Teachers from ethnic minorities have first hand experience of racism in their own lives in the mainstream school system. The work of Pole (2001) and also Osler (1997) noted the impact of the formal and hidden curriculum on student teachers. 'The experience involved teachers coping and overcoming different forms of racism in the curriculum, pedagogy and school organisation' (Poole, 2001). It is this relationship that drives the recurring demand for more ethnic minority teachers in mainstream schools.

The necessity for the whole curriculum to be relevant to children's cultural experiences is widely acknowledged in mainstream education. In successful complementary schools both language and culturally relevant curriculum are utilised to make learning more relevant to black and linguistic minority children. In some complementary schools cultural values, attitudes and expectations are transmitted mainly through interaction between the staff or other adults and the pupils at the schools, and by their positions within the community.

The advantageous small class sizes are key to teachers knowing and meeting children's differing learning needs. Knowledgeable teachers who are versed in the languages, customs and expectations of the children's communities help establish and maintain close working relationships with parents. Most complementary schools' staff have endured and have first hand experience and understanding of racism. They know how racism operates within education to disenfranchise minority children. The ability of teachers and communities to construct small *habitus*, pockets of shared cultural knowledge within the domain of education, is a valuable characteristic of complementary education.

Implications for the TDA and training institutions

The Training and Development Agency publishes annual figures showing how well NQTs think their training institutions have prepared them for the classroom. There is always a question about preparation for teaching in multicultural schools – and every year only about one third of the NQTs say that they feel that this has been adequately addressed in their course. Our recommendations, therefore, are that:

- ITT institutions should prepare *all* teachers to be able to teach *all* children. Teachers should understand how institutional racism operates in society and specifically in education and how racism impinges on ethnic minority children's lives in school

- As urged by Wanless (2007), educators should know, respect and share the ambitions and expectations for their children's education of the parents and community so that parents, community and school can work in partnership

■ Initial teacher training agencies and curriculum providers must make the curriculum culturally and linguistically relevant to all children

■ Teachers from minority communities who know and understand their communities and have shared cultural values, expectations and aspirations should be employed as initial teacher trainers. Their experience should be taken as the starting point for the student teachers

■ Small classes facilitate learning and keep it dynamic and this should be borne in mind by the DCSF

■ Teachers in complementary schools working with reception and KS1 children could improve their effectiveness by using more interactive teaching resources

■ Mainstream schools should be more generous about sharing their resources with the complementary schools which use their premises

■ The DCSF should work with local authorities to foster and support partnerships between mainstream and complementary schools

These findings are especially timely when the Government is rethinking its key strategies in education. Lord Dearing, who chaired the review of languages in 2006 described community languages as a 'national asset'. The present government supported investigation was the most extensive since the Bullock Report in 1975. In the *Key Stage 2 Framework for Languages* an integrationist approach to language learning is promoted through topic based learning in KS2. Children's learning of languages is seen as part of their overall learning in the classroom and pupils' skills and knowledge in community languages are regarded as being as important as in English.

Every Language Matters (Ofsted, 2008) sought to assess the quality of initial teacher training in languages other than French, German, Irish, Spanish and Welsh. The report was produced at a time when the number of pupils taking languages at GCSE level was falling, even though schools are being encouraged to take on a wider range of world languages. It described good practice in training and teaching. The Ofsted survey was set against a background of inspection which showed consistently high results in community languages at GCSE and yet a wide variation in the quality of teaching. Its findings revealed the difficulties ITT institutions faced when offering community languages. The main issue was seen as finding suitable school placements (2008: 6). Supporting PGCE courses in community languages at higher education institutes will further encourage secondary students to enter for GCSEs in their community languages.

Every Language Matters highlighted important issues relating to the role of the teacher training institutions. For a start, the most effective PGCE courses had skilled tutors who were specialists in the languages the student teachers were intending to teach and gave them additional training in the relevant language. Secondly, not all the information about languages taught in schools was made readily available to providers, so adding to the difficulties of finding suitable placements for prospective student teachers and causing at least one provider to turn down applicants who actually met all the criteria for admission to the course. Neither was information about PGCE courses for community languages always clear, and in some cases it was contradictory.

Ofsted drew attention to some of the challenges facing prospective teachers which kept out many candidates:

- would-be PGCE students wishing to follow courses in community languages faced significant barriers
- the range of languages offered was inadequate
- the location of the training was difficult to access
- the requirement that they should also be able to teach a European language to at least KS 3 kept out many candidates.

This contrasted with Ofsted's findings on community language teaching in schools, which were generally positive. The quality of teaching by teachers who had a PGCE in community languages was consistently good. Their teaching was characterised by detailed planning, good provision for different groups, good knowledge of ICT and stimulating activities that engaged and enthused learners.

Some programmes, which were also highlighted in the CILT report, provided good alternative routes into teaching. The graduate teacher programme offered a successful employment-based route into teaching. However, five of the sixteen teachers in the survey who trained via this route had to qualify to teach a subject other than a community language because no one was available to assess them (Ofsted, 2008:7).

The Ofsted report's recommendations provided a sound framework for supporting community language teaching. Its strength was its multi-agency approach:

The Department for Children, Schools and Families (DCSF) was called on to:

■ provide a wider range of national web-based resources for languages beyond French, German and Spanish.

The Training and Development Agency for Schools (TDA) was asked to:

■ ensure that all community languages teachers have the opportunity to achieve qualified teacher status

■ provide clear guidance to ITT institutions on how to make flexible courses available to PGCE languages applicants

■ consider how PGCE language courses might offer a wider range of languages than French, German and Spanish and how to accord equal status to all of them

■ review how PGCE courses are advertised and ensure that communities are better informed about the courses offered. (Ofsted, 2008:7)

Ofsted recommended that providers of **Initial Teacher Training** should:

■ review admissions criteria so that PGCE language courses could admit applicants without a European language

■ ensure that PGCE courses provide specific language skills training alongside generic training

■ Ensure that they (ITT institutions) are well informed about which languages are taught in schools, so that partner schools can offer a wider range of languages in placements.

Time after time the Government stresses the need for children to reach their full potential. Welcome as this statement of aim is, it can only be achieved if all agencies are committed to making it happen. We feel this can be done through a dialogical approach at both macro and micro levels. First of all a proactive strategy needs to be led by the government and this can be achieved through the government's *Every Child Matters* agenda. As this book has shown, complementary schools perform a multiplicity of valuable functions and will be compatible with the multi-agency approach advocated by government. Both sectors, the mainstream and the complementary, will greatly benefit from close co-operation. The latter will provide a wealth of positive practice relating to how minority children's language, culture and identity can be utilised in their learning. And mainstream schools will acquire insights into the 'missing link' – the part of minority children's learning they have so far left untouched.

But how will this be achieved? First of all it would be naïve to assume that the government's commitment and improved funding could on its own achieve such integration. The local authorities also have a major role. Their task is not easy, since schools enjoy semi-independent status but most LAs still retain – albeit shrinking – Ethnic Minority Achievement (EMA) Services. It is through these services that most LAs maintain contact with the complementary schools in their borough or county. One such authority, Hackney, has maintained excellent links with its complementary schools, organising training for complementary school teachers through close links with the National Resource Centre for Supplementary Schools. The Complementary Schools unit worked closely with the EMA team to establish contacts between mainstream and complementary schools. We think that the vital linking role of this service is not fully utilised elsewhere and that all LAs need to follow Hackney's example.

The other important area to consider is research. Although there are an increasing number of research projects relating to complementary schools (Abdelrazak, 2001; Creese *et al*, 2007; CILT, 2008; Lytra and Martin, forthcoming, 2009), there is an urgent need for extensive research backed by the government.

The DCSF is currently funding a research project exploring the impact of complementary schools on the academic attainment of their pupils in their education in the mainstream. This is being carried out by IPSE, the Institute of Policy Studies in Education at London Metropolitan University, and the National Centre for Social Research. www.london met.ac.uk/research-units/ipse www.natcen.ac.uk

These studies of complementary schools indicate clearly and un-equivocally that they need to be fully integrated into the new multi-agency structure of provision for children. Not only do these schools foster the identity formation and self esteem of children that is vital for learning but they also offer important linguistic and cultural experiences to enhance children's potential to achieve optimal educational success.

List of Acronyms

CECWA	Caribbean Education and Community Workers Association.
CILT	The National Centre for Languages
CL	Community Language
CRB	Criminal Records Bureau
DCSF	Department for Children, Schools and Families
DfES	Department for Education and Skills
EEC	European Economic Community
EMA	Ethnic Minority Achievement
GCSE	General Certificate of Secondary Education
GNVQ	General National Vocational Qualification
GTP	Graduate Teachers Programme
ICT	Information and Communication Technology
IELTS	International English Language Testing System
ILEA	Inner London Education Authority
ITE	Initial Teacher Education
ITT	Initial Teacher Education
KS1	Key Stage One
KS3	Key Stage Three
LA	Local Authority
LMS	Local Management of Schools
NC	National Curriculum
NRC	The National Resource Centre
NLWIA	North London West Indian Association
OTT	Overseas Trained Teacher
PGCE	Post Graduate Certificate in Education
QCA	Qualifications and Curriculum Authority
QTS	Qualified Teacher Status
RE	Religious Education
RTP	Registered Teachers Programme
TDA	Training and Development Agency

Appendix 1
The London Complementary
Schools Questionnaire
and some answers

Camden → United Reform Church Multiple
Buck Street Purpose
NW1 8NJ.

Holy name

Complimentary Schools' Questionnaire

1

Name of school/Contact person	Camden Chinese Community Centre nursery
Why and When was the school started	1986

Camden
United
Reform Church
Buck Sheet
NW1 8NJ

1 yr	3 yrs	Longer (please state number of years)
		✓

2 How many teaching staff are they in the school?

4

3. How many volunteers do you have in your school?

0

4. What type of training or qualification do members of staff in your school have? Please give numbers in boxes below

Overseas qualification or training	Other
2	

UK Qualified Teacher Status	Other
1	

5. What additional training do you provide for teachers?

Camden Early Years Training

6. What kind of curriculum is on offer to the children? (You may tick more than one box)

Mother tongue teaching/community language

[✓]

National curriculum support i.e. English, Maths, Science

[✓]

Religious education

[ ]

Afro-Centric i.e. Black history/culture?

[ ]

7 a) How many children attend your school?

Numbers

Male	Female	Age range
11	7	2~5 years

b) Which age ranges do you cater for? (please give approximate numbers)

Pre-school (3-5)	Primary (5-11)	Secondary (11-16)	16+
✓			

8. What are the nationalities, cultural or ethnic heritage of children attending your school?

Chinese 5
Chinese mixed 6.
French. Italian, African 7
English, Kosova.

Christian
Catholic
Buddhist

8 Which main community groups does your school serve?

Chinese

2

151

9 How often does the school function? (State which days)

Weekdays	Weekends	Other
Mon — Fri. 5 days		

10 Which of these categories would best describe your school's ethos?

Language	Religious	Tutorial	Other (please state)
✓			

11 Would you please indicate whether we can visit your school

Yes	No
✓	

Contact Name: [REMOVED FOR PRIVACY]

Tel No:

Thank you for your time. If you have any further questions or comments please continue on the reverse or add a page or call:

Tözün Issa   or Claudette Williams

Please return completed application forms to:
T. Issa and C. Willams
Complementary Schools' Project
London Metropolitan University
Department of Education
166-220 Holloway Road
London N7 8DB

3

Appendix 2
The CILT Questionnaires for teachers and headteachers

Appendix 2
CILT Survey

Supplementary Schools: Survey of Teachers

The National Resource Centre for Supplementary Education have asked us to find out about the needs of teachers in supplementary schools, and how many wish to obtain UK Qualified Teaching Status (QTS). We would be grateful if you could answer these questions and return the form to us in the FREEPOST envelope provided by **January 25th**.

Your answers will be confidential and anonymous. We hope you are able to complete the questionnaire, but you do not need to respond to any questions you are uncomfortable with.

Section 1: About the school you work in

1. **Name of your school:** ....

   (You do not have to give the name if you do not wish to)

2. **Where is your supplementary school?** *(please tick):*

   ☐ Islington ☐ Kensington & Chelsea ☐ Westminster ☐ Camden ☐ Hackney ☐ Haringey ☐ Waltham Forest

3. **Which of the following does your school cover?** (please tick all that apply):

   ☐ National Curriculum ☐ Mother Tongue ☐ Culture & Heritage ☐ Religious Studies ☐ Other

4. **What subject(s) do you teach at this school?** *(please list all that you teach)*:

   ....

5. **Which age groups do you teach?** *(choose one or more of the following)*

   Under 5 ☐   5-11 ☐   11-16 ☐   16-18 ☐   Adults ☐

6. **Do you teach....?**

   Boys and girls ☐   Boys only ☐   Girls only ☐

7. **When do you teach at this school?** *Please tick all that apply*

   After school ☐   Saturdays ☐   Sundays ☐

8. **How many hours a week do you normally teach at this school?** .... hours

9. **How long have you taught at this school for?** .... years

Section 2: About your educational qualifications and experience

10. **What educational qualifications do you have?** *Please complete the table*

Type of qualification	Tick all that apply	Year obtained	Country obtained
First degree (e.g. B.A., Baccalaureate)			
Post graduate (e.g. Master's, PhD)			
Teaching qualification			
GCSE's/ A levels (or equivalent)			

Other, please specify below (e.g. diploma)
....

1

11. Do you hold a UK Qualified Teacher Status (QTS) teaching qualification?

Yes ☐ ⟶ **What year did you qualify?** ....

No ☐ ⟶ **Have you ever attempted to gain QTS?** Yes ☐ No ☐

12. **Do you have any qualifications to teach language(s)?** Yes ☐ No ☐

If **YES**, please indicate the languages you are qualified to teach:

....

13. **Do you have any teaching experience outside of the UK?**

No ☐ | Go to Section 3 ⟩

Yes ☐ ⟶ **How many years teaching experience do you have?** ....yrs

14. **Please specify which country/countries you gained your teaching experience in:**

....

15. **Where did you teach?**

☐	☐	☐	☐	☐
Primary school	Secondary school	College	University	Other

If other, please give further details: ....

16. **What was your position and responsibility in the school/institution?**

☐	☐	☐	☐
Teacher	Headteacher	Lecturer	Other

If other, please give further details: ....

17. **What subject(s) did you teach?** *Please tick all that apply*

☐	☐	☐	☐	☐	☐	☐
Mathematics	Sciences	Languages	Humanities / Social Studies	Religious studies	ICT	Other

If languages, or other, please give further details:...... ....

Section 3: About obtaining UK Qualified Teacher Status (QTS)

18. **Would you like to obtain UK QTS?**

Yes ☐ Go to Question 19

No ☐ Why not?

....
.... | Go to Section 5 ⟩

I already have UK ☐ | Go to Section 5 ⟩
QTS

2

19. Do you agree or disagree with the following statements about why you are interested in obtaining UK QTS?

	Agree	Disagree	Neither agree nor disagree
I think it would enhance my job prospects	☐	☐	☐
I would like to teach in mainstream schools	☐	☐	☐
I think it would help me to teach my subject area better	☐	☐	☐
It provides an opportunity to obtain a UK qualification	☐	☐	☐

Other, please specify ....

20. Where would you would like to teach in when you obtain QTS

☐	☐	☐	☐	☐
Early Years' Settings	Primary schools	Secondary schools	Further Education	Other

21. What subject (s) would you like to teach if you get UK QTS?

☐	☐	☐	☐	☐	☐	☐
Mathematics	Sciences	Languages	Humanities / Social Studies	Religious studies	ICT	Other

If **languages**, or **other**, please give further details: ....

Section 4: About additional skills needed to obtain UK QTS

22. To what extent do you agree with the following statements about the perceived barriers to enrolling on a QTS course?

	Agree	Disagree	Neither agree nor disagree
I don't think my prior qualifications and experience will be recognised	☐	☐	☐
I don't think funding is available	☐	☐	☐
My immigration status/work permit will not allow me to study	☐	☐	☐
The courses are not flexible enough	☐	☐	☐
I have other work commitments	☐	☐	☐
My family responsibilities take up all my time	☐	☐	☐

Other please specify:..

23. Please indicate to what extent you think you need the following additional skills to begin a UK QTS course?

	Agree	Disagree	Neither agree nor disagree
I think I need to improve my maths	☐	☐	☐
I need to improve my proficiency in English	☐	☐	☐
I need to develop my ICT knowledge	☐	☐	☐
I need to improve my proficiency in the language(s) I want to teach	☐	☐	☐
I need to learn about the English system of education	☐	☐	☐

Other, please specify: ....

3

Section 5: About you

This section asks a few questions about your background. This helps us understand more about those who teach in supplementary schools.

24. Which age group are you in?

☐	☐	☐	☐	☐	☐	☐	☐	☐
Under 25	25- 29	30-34	35-39	40-44	45-49	50-54	55-60	Over 60

25. Are you: ☐ Male or   ☐ Female?

26. How would you describe your ethnic background? ....

27. Tick the boxes to show the languages in which you feel you are competent in

(a) **speaking**   (b) **reading**   and   (c) **writing**   (*write in all your languages*)

Language	Speaking			Reading			Writing		
	very fluent	fairly fluent	a little	very strong	fair understanding	some understanding	advanced ability	fair ability	moderate ability
English									
....									
....									
....									
....									

28. In which country were you born? ....

29. What is your nationality? ....

---

30. Would you be interested in following a preparatory course for QTS in the local area?

Yes   ☐   No   ☐

31. Would you be interested in taking part in a small group discussion about issues raised in this survey (at a time convenient to you)?

Yes   ☐   No   ☐

(if you answered **YES** to either **Q30 or Q31** above, please can we have your name and either a phone number or e-mail, so we can contact you)

Name .... Contact e-mail/phone...

....

*If you know of a colleague(s) in a supplementary school in North London who might be interested in participating in this research, please pass on their contact details to us or ask them to contact us at ipse@londonmet.ac.uk so that we can send them a copy of the questionnaire.

Thank you. Please return your completed questionnaire in the envelope provided to FREEPOST, LON 18903, IPSE, London Metropolitan University, 166-220 Holloway Road, London N7 8DB by 25 January 2008.

Λ

Supplementary Schools: Survey of Headteachers

The National Resource Centre for Supplementary Education have asked us to find out about the needs of teachers in supplementary schools. We would be grateful if you could answer these questions and return the form to us by **January 25th 2008.** If you teach in your school, please also complete the **Teacher Survey.**

Your answers will be confidential and anonymous. We hope you are able to complete the questionnaire, but you do not need to respond to any questions you are uncomfortable with.

Section 1: Your School

1. Name of your school: ....
   (You do not have to give the name if you do not wish to)

2. How many pupils are in your school?
   Less than 25 ☐   25-50 ☐   50-100 ☐   More than 100 ☐

3. Which age groups are taught in your school? *(choose one or more of the following)*
   Under 5 ☐   5-11 ☐   11-16 ☐   16-18 ☐   Adults ☐

4. How are children taught?
   By age ☐   By ability ☐   Language competence ☐   Other ☐

5. Does the school serve a particular community?
   Yes ☐   **Which community?** ....
   No ☐

6. Where is your supplementary school? *(please tick):*

☐	☐	☐	☐	☐	☐	☐
Islington	Kensington & Chelsea	Westminster	Camden	Hackney	Haringey	Waltham Forest

7. Which geographical area(s) does your school serve? ....

8. What language(s) are taught at your school? *Please specify* ....
....

9. Which of the following does your school cover? *(please tick all that apply)*:

☐	☐	☐	☐	☐
National Curriculum	Mother Tongue	Culture & Heritage	Religious Studies	Other

If other, please specify: ....

10. If National Curriculum is taught, which of the following subjects are covered?

☐	☐	☐	☐	☐
Maths	English	Sciences	Languages	Other

If other, please specify: ....

5

Section 2: *Your Teachers*

11. How many teachers work at your school? ....

12. How many of your teachers currently have UK QTS? ....

13. Do you think any of your teachers who do not have UK QTS would like to gain it in the future?

        Yes ☐   No ☐   Don't know ☐

14. How long do teachers usually teach for at the school?

☐	☐	☐	☐
Less than 1 year	1-2 years	3-5 years	5 years or more

15. To what extent do you agree with the following statements about teacher recruitment to your school?

	Agree	Disagree	Neither agree nor disagree
I do not have a problem recruiting teachers	☐	☐	☐
There are a lack of language specialists	☐	☐	☐
I can only afford to employ a small number of staff	☐	☐	☐
There are a shortage of teachers with qualifications	☐	☐	☐
I don't have sufficient resources to take on more classes	☐	☐	☐
Our school times make it difficult to recruit teachers because of their work and family commitments	☐	☐	☐
The location of my school makes it difficult to attract staff	☐	☐	☐
Those who apply do not have sufficient training/experience	☐	☐	☐

Are there any other factors that make recruitment difficult?...

16. To what extent do you agree with the following statements about teacher retention in your school?

	Agree	Disagree	Neither agree nor disagree
I have no problem retaining teachers in my school	☐	☐	☐
I lose teachers to mainstream schools	☐	☐	☐
Teachers leave to concentrate on other commitments	☐	☐	☐
A heavy workload discourages teachers from staying	☐	☐	☐
Teachers leave to other work, or to develop other skills	☐	☐	☐
Insufficient funding makes it difficult to retain teachers	☐	☐	☐
Teachers leave because we do not have up-to-date resources	☐	☐	☐

Are there any other difficulties in retaining staff? ....

17. To what extent do you agree with the following statements?

	Agree	Disagree	Neither agree nor disagree
My teachers would leave as soon as they acquire UK QTS	☐	☐	☐
It would be good for my school if more teachers had UK QTS	☐	☐	☐

Thank you. Please return your completed questionnaire in the envelope provided to FREEPOST, LON 18903, IPSE, London Metropolitan University, 166-220 Holloway Road, London N7 8DB by 25 January 2008

6

References

Abdelrazak, M. (2001) *Supplementary and Mother tongue schools in England*, London: DfES

Adonis, A. (2006) 'Supporting role' in *Education Guardian* 26 April

Bourdieu, P. (1986) *The Field of Cultural Production*, Cambridge: Polity Press

Brown, W. (2005) The future before us, p 72 -76, in Richardson, B (ed) *Tell it Like it is: how our schools fail Black children*, London: Bookmarks Publications and Trentham

Bryant, B, Dadzie, S and Scafe, S (1985) *The Heart of the Race: Black Women's Lives in Britain*, London: Virago

Bushell, W. (1969) 'Proposal for North London West Indian Association, concerning education in Haringey, George Padmore Institute; Ref BEM1/2/5:Sheet 25-27, Paper 3. Stroud Green Road, London N7

Callender, C. (1997) *Education for Empowerment: The practice and philosophy of Black Teachers.* Stoke on Trent: Trentham

CILT, the National Centre for Languages (2008) *Our Languages: Teachers in Supplementary Schools and their Aspirations to Teach Community Languages*, London: CILT.

Coard, B. (1971) *How the West Indian Child is Made Educationally Subnormal in the British School System.* London: New Beacon

Creese, A., Lytra,V., Baraç, T, Yağcıoğlu-Ali, D. (2007) *Investigating Multilingualism in Turkish complementary schools in London,* University of Birmingham

Curtis, P. (2008) 'Education: Black Caribbean children held back by institutional racism in schools', *Education Guardian*, 5 September

Dabydeen, D. (1985) *The Black Presence in English Literature,* Manchester University Press

Dabydeen, D. (1987) *Hogarth's Black: Images of Blacks in Eighteen Century Art*, Manchester University Press

Dabydeen, D. (1994) *Letters of Ignatius Sancho,* Edinburgh University Press

DES (1967) *Children and their Primary Schools: A Report of the Central Advisory Council for Education (England) the Plowden Report*, London, HMSO

DES (1975) *Language for Life: Report of the Committee of Inquiry, The Bullock Report,* London, HMSO

Desai, R. (1963) *Indian Immigrants in Britain,* Oxford: Oxford university Press

Doulton, A. (1969) 'Banding and the Immigrant Child' Report to Haringey's Education Committee January 13, para 5E-para 11 p17

Employability Forum (2006) Report of the Refugee Teachers Task Force: 'Opening doors for refugees working in education', London: Regents' College.

Fitzpatrick, F (1987) *The Open Door,* Bradford Mother Tongue Project. Clevedon: Multilingual Matters

Fryer, P. (1984) *Staying power: The history of black people in Britain,* London: Pluto Press

Gilborn, D and Mirza, H. S, (2000) *Educational Inequality: Mapping Race, Class and Gender – A synthesis of research evidence,* HMI 232 London, Stationery Office

Gregory, E. and Williams, A. (2000) *City Literacies: Learning to Read Across Generations and Cultures,* London: Routledge

Guardian Unlimited (2006) 'Supporting role' 26 April

Haxell, M. A. (1979) 'European Immigration and Bradford'. Unpublished paper. Bradford and Ilkley Community College, West Yorkshire

Home Office (1962) *Commonwealth Immigrants Act: Control of Immigration Statistics 1962/1963/1966,* Home Office (Cmnd. 2151, 2379,2658, 2979, 3258) London: HMSO

Issa, T. (2002) 'Augmentation of Language and Thinking in Bilingual Children, Unpublished PhD Thesis, University of North London

Issa, T. (2005) *Talking Turkey: the language, culture and identity of Turkish speaking children in Britain,* Stoke on Trent: Trentham

John, G. (2006) *Taking a Stand,* Manchester: The Gus John Partnership Ltd

Jones, J. (1977) *The Human Face of Labour.* London: British Broadcasting Corporation

Kenner, C. (2004) *Becoming Biliterate, Young Children Learning Different Writing Systems,* Stoke on Trent: Trentham

Khan, N. (1976) *The Arts Britain Ignores: the arts of ethnic minorities in Britain,* London: CRE

Khan, V.S. (1980) The Mother Tongue of Linguistic Minorities in England, *Journal of Multilingual and Multicultural Development,* 1(1): 71-88

King, R.L (1977) 'Italian migration to Great Britain', *Geography,* 62(3): 176-86

Klein, G. (1982) *Resources for Education in Multicultural Society.* York: Longmans for Schools Council

Levy, A. (2005) *Small Island.* London: *Guardian,* Headline Review

Lytra, V. and Martin, P. (2009 forthcoming) *Sites of Multilingualism: Complementary schools in Britain today.* Stoke on Trent: Trentham.

Macpherson, W. (1999) *The Stephen Lawrence Inquiry,* Report, London, Stationery Office

REFERENCES

Martin, P.W., A. Bhatt, N. Bhojani and A. Creese (2004) A Final Report on Complementary Schools and their Communities in Leicester. University of Leicester/University of Birmingham. (ESRC R000223949)

Rampton, A. (1981) *West Indian Children in Our Schools,* London HMSO

Reay, D. and Mirza, H.S. (1996) *Uncovering Genealogies of the Margins*, Manchester University Press

Ofsted (2005) *Race Equality in Education: Good practice in Schools and Local Education Authorities.* HMI Report 2398

Ofsted (2008) *Every Language Matters,* London: Ofsted

Osler, A. (1997) *The Education Career of Black Teachers: Changing Identities, Changing Lives,* Buckingham, Open University Press

Perkins, T., Isha Mavinga McKenzie (1992) *In search of Mr McKenzie: Two sisters' quest for an unknown father,* London, Women's Press

Philips, M. and Philips, T. (1998) *Windrush: the irresistible rise of multi-racial Britain,* London, Harper Collins

Pole, C. (2001) Black Teachers: Curriculum and Career in *The Curriculum Journal* 12(3)

Richardson, B. (2005) (ed) *Tell it Like it is: How Our Schools Fail Black Children,* London: Bookmarks Publications and Trentham Books

Robertson, L. (2006) *The Role of Community Groups and Community Language Schools.* London: Multiverse p28

Rodgers, J.A. (1970) *Sex and Race: Negro-Caucasian Mixing in All Ages and All Lands: The Old World,* Helga M. Rogers USA, Studies in Imperialism

Schwarz, B.(ed) (2003) *West Indian Intellectuals in Britain,* Manchester University Press

Seacole, M. (1990, originally published 1857) *The Wonderful Adventure of Mrs Seacole in Many Lands,* Oxford University Press

Searle, C. (2005) 'A vital Instrument' in Richardson (ed) *op cit,* Bookmarks

Sherwood, K. (2007) Slavery Justice: Lord Mansfield and Dido Belle at Kenwood (29 May) 24hoursmuseum.org

Simon, D. (2005) 'Education for the Blacks: the supplementary school movement' in Richardson, B. (Ed) *op cit*

Stubbs, M. (ed.) (1985) *The Other Languages of England: Linguistic Minorities Project.* London: Routledge.

Swann, M. (1985) *Education for All: Final Report of the Committee of Inquiry Into the Education of Children from Ethnic Minority Groups.* London: HMSO.

Tansley, P. (1986) *Community Languages in Primary Education* Report from the SCDC Mother Tongue Project. Windsor: NFER-Nelson

Taylor, J. M. (1976) *Sikhs in Britain: An Annotated Bibliography,* Coventry: Centre for Research in Ethnic Relations, University of Warwick

Taylor, M. J. (1988) *Between Two Cultures,* Slough: NFER-Nelson

Vertovec, S. (1993) 'Indo-Caribbean Experience in Britain: Overlooked, Miscate-gorised, Misunderstood' in James, W and Harris, C. (eds) *Inside Babylon the Caribbean Diaspora in Britain,* London: Verson

Visram, R. (1993) 'South Asians in London' in Merriman, N (ed) *The Peopling of London: Fifteen Thousand Years of Settlement from Overseas,* Museum of London

Walker, I. (1982) 'Garibaldi was here', *Observer* [suppl] 4 April

Wanless, P. (2007) Priority Review: Exclusion of Black Pupils 'Getting it. Getting it right' DfES. Available at: http://www.standards.dfes.gov.uk/ethnicminorities/ resources/ PriorityReviewSept06.pdf

Winder, R. (2004) *Bloody Foreigners: The Story of Immigration into Britain,* London: Little Brown.

Index